A WOK FOR ALL SEASONS

A WOK FOR ALL SEASONS

MARTIN YAN

Doubleday

NEW YORK   LONDON   TORONTO   SYDNEY   AUCKLAND

Managing Editor: Jay Harlow

Text and Research Contributors:

Diane Oda	Carrie Seeman
Jan Nix	Gladys Lee
Dorthy Lee	Gail Ellerbrake
Lena Fong	Shirley Fong-Torres
Susan Yan	Ivan Lai

Designer: Salinda Tyson

Photography and page layout: Larry Guyer and Steve Larson,
The Graphic Marketing Group

Food Stylist: Joanne Dexter

Illustrator: Pauline Phung

Color Printing Coordinator: Interprint

Props for Photography and Yan Can Cook Show:
Takahashi, San Francisco
Emporium-Capwell, San Francisco

Published by Doubleday, a division of Bantam Doubleday Dell Publishing
Group, Inc. 666 Fifth Avenue, New York, New York 10103

Library of Congress Cataloging-in-Publication Data:

Yan, Martin
    A wok for all seasons.

    Includes index.
    1. Cookery, Chinese.   1. Title
TX724.5.C5Y284   1988   641.5951   88-20351

ISBN 0-385-24386-3

CONTENTS

Index of Shows

Acknowledgements

"Never have so few owed so much to so many." I often think of this saying and how appropriately it describes my life during these past months, with the production of the YAN CAN COOK shows and *A Wok For All Seasons*.

Producing a television show is for me an enlightening and humbling experience. I soon learned to appreciate the complexity of the business and the need to pool many talents. My deepest gratitude, therefore, must first go to Marjorie Poore, my executive producer at KQED, San Francisco, who spearheaded the entire project; and to Gayle Yamada, senior producer; to Donna Miller, producer; to Katherine Russell, director; and to every single member of our top-notch production crew.

In making various points of transition on screen, I habitually referred to the phrase "the magic of television." The true magician in this case is Linda Brandt. She and the entire supporting team in the back kitchen, Carrie, Rhoda, Gladys, Vivienne, and Bernice, are the ones who made it appear so smooth and effortless on camera. And the script helped. Ivan Lai managed to punch up lively situations where I could be at my best.

I was privileged to have as guests famous chefs and food professionals such as Chef Larry Chu (Chef Chu's Restaurant), Jay Harlow ("The Fishmonger" columnist for the *San Francisco Chronicle*), and T.J. Robinson (Gingerbread House Restaurant). I want to thank especially my good friend, French master chef Jacques Pepin, who took time off his busy schedule and let me share his spotlight.

For the completion of *A Wok For All Seasons*, I am forever indebted to Alison Brown Cerier, Joel Fishman, Les Pockell, and their colleagues at Doubleday, and to the many talented individuals who have contributed their time and effort.

On the more personal side, I must thank Rocky and Irma Kalish, who have lent me their creative energy to all my projects; and of course Sue, whose patience and support form the basic foundation for all my endeavors.

Finally, to all of you out there, my readers and viewers. Together with my mother, you are my greatest inspiration.

Introduction

Teaching cooking and writing about cooking is a two-way street. For all the years that I have been teaching Chinese cooking in person and on television, I have also been learning, absorbing new ideas from Western cuisines into my own personal cooking style. These ideas come from many sources — questions and suggestions from students, viewers, readers, and my colleagues, among whom I particularly want to thank Jacques Pepin, Julia Child, Jeff Smith, and Nathalie Dupree for their friendship and encouragement.

Of course, I still practice and teach the classic Chinese techniques and dishes I learned when growing up. Whenever I travel, both in North America and in the Orient, I take every opportunity to work alongside Chinese master chefs, gaining new insights into the ancient traditions of Chinese cooking and observing how the cuisine evolves as it incorporates new ideas and new foods.

Like restaurant chefs, home cooks today have a much greater range of ingredients and flavors to choose from in creating Chinese dishes and menus. This kind of contemporary, internationally inspired Chinese cooking is the subject of the seventh season of YAN CAN COOK on public television, and of this new collection of recipes, *A Wok for All Seasons*.

The shows on this year's series have been organized around a single theme, such as Harvest from the Garden (an assortment of seasonal vegetable dishes) or My Mom's Favorites, some of the dishes I grew up loving. There are also shows on how to Cook Ahead, or what to do when you have No Time to Shop. There is a special romantic Dinner for Two, plus a Dinner for Four, A Banquet Experience, and A Chinese Picnic. Every recipe featured in the shows appears in this book; for those who want to follow along with the recipes while watching, the Index of Shows on pages 6 and 7 will refer you to the location of each week's recipes.

Western cooks no longer need to be told that Chinese cooking is healthful, simple (in most cases), and generally perfect for today's active, nutrition-conscious lifestyle. It also tastes good! No wonder Oriental ingredients such as ginger, soy sauce, enoki mushrooms, and Cantonese fermented black beans are showing up on many Western menus these days. At the same time, Chinese cooks are expanding the boundaries of the cuisine, incorporating ingredients like milk, cream, and salad dressings that are nearly unknown in traditional Chinese cooking.

I invite you to join in the process, and offer this collection of recipes for both traditional and innovative Chinese dishes to add to your international repertoire. Once you understand the basics — and by preparing the recipes in this book you will learn the basic principles underlying this ancient and complex cuisine — all you need is imagination. Remember — If Yan Can Cook, So Can You!

I have been "into" woks since I was a child.

Cooking Utensils and Tools

The Wok: Curved like a shallow bowl, the wok is the most important utensil used for Chinese cooking. There are round and flat-bottomed woks, the former being the most traditional and efficient, and the latter designed more recently for electric stoves.

Round and flat-bottomed woks are made of spun carbon steel, stainless steel, or aluminum and stainless steel (often with copper sides and bottom). The spun steel is the most common since it retains high temperatures and conducts heat evenly, yet is reasonably priced. The latest arrivals are woks made from hard-anodized aluminum; they require no seasoning and are scratch-resistant — they do not react with food, either. You can also find a quality and long-lasting nonstick wok, "Circulon," which has a 10-year warranty.

Most woks are available in diameters from 12, 14, 16, and up to 24 inches. The 14-inch is ideal for home use and will accommodate recipes for 2 to 6 servings. The handle design is also a matter of choice — two metal ones, or one long handle.

If your preference is for an electric wok, you can choose among nonstick, stainless steel, or the newest ones made from hard-anodized aluminum. Most of these are adequate for deep-frying or tabletop cooking, but generally are not hot enough for stir-frying, as they do not reach as high a temperature as a wok placed on a gas stove. Most electric woks are 1100 watts; if you can find a 1500-watt Proforge electric wok (manufactured by Meyer), it should do the job. A good electric wok has one major advantage over the stovetop woks; you can cook with it anywhere with a perfect control of cooking temperature.

Spun-steel woks last a long time with a little simple maintenance. A new one should be scoured with hot, soapy water to remove any protective coating applied at the factory. Dry the wok thoroughly, rub some vegetable oil evenly into the cooking surface, and heat until the inner surface turns brown. This builds the first layer of a "seasoned" surface and keeps food from sticking during high heat cooking. (Woks may vary so please follow manufacturer's directions.) After each use, wash the wok with hot water (very little or no soap), dry well, and rub in a bit of fresh oil.

Wok Accessories: Most woks come with a standard set of accessories. A tight-fitting lid, usually made of aluminum or stainless steel, is essential for steaming. A ring stand provides a secure base for round-bottomed woks and is especially important when steaming or deep-frying. The long-handled Chinese spatula is shaped like a small shovel with a curved edge to match the curvature of the wok. It is used for tossing, scooping, and retrieving food in a wok. The ladle, less functional, is used to dip and scoop large amounts of cooked food and liquid to serving dishes. Wire strainers of coarsely woven brass come in a variety of sizes and are used to gather and transfer foods quickly from hot oil or boiling water.

Steamers: Whether made of bamboo or aluminum, stackable steamers allow one or more dishes to be cooked over a wok of boiling water. The traditional bamboo version is preferable to the aluminum model for steaming buns or dumplings; its lattice top allows extra steam to dissipate, which prevents excessive condensation from dripping onto the food.

Another method of steaming is to put the food on a plate set on top of a steaming rack inside the wok, or simply place two pairs of chopsticks, tic-tac-toe style, over boiling water as an improvised rack. There are several designs of racks on the market, from pedestals to perforated trays.

Clay Pots: Also known as "sand pots" due to the color and texture of the unglazed exterior, these traditional earthenware cooking pots are used to produce rich, concentrated, slow-cooking braised dishes. There are a variety of shapes and sizes, all with lids, and typically glazed on the inside only. Some are encased in a wire frame for added protection. Take care never to place a cold empty pot directly on heat, or a hot pot on a cold surface. Substitute any flameproof covered casserole.

The Cleaver (Chinese Chef's Knife): Like the wok, the large, wide-bladed Chinese chef's knife is multi-functional. You can use it to slice, dice, shred, and mince, to tenderize meat, or to crush. The broad blade also serves as a scoop to lift chopped food from the cutting board to the pan. Always keep the edge sharp. After each use, wipe the blade with a hot soapy cloth, rinse and wipe dry. The Chinese chef's knife may feel a bit large and awkward the first time you hold it. Go slowly while you develop your skill, and with a few weeks practice, you will be slicing and dicing with ease. Note: Most Chinese chef's knives are not designed for chopping meats through the bone. Use a real meat cleaver or let your butcher do it for you.

Cutting Techniques

Holding the Cleaver: Hold the handle and slide your hand forward just until your thumb reaches one side of the blade and your index finger is on the other side. Grip the handle tightly. Curl the fingers of your other hand inward and press down on the food to be cut. Use the first knuckle as a cutting guide for the blade.

Slicing: Whether slicing straight across or diagonally, hold the food as above and cut straight down with the blade. Slicing stalk-like or cylindrical vegetables (such as celery, carrots, or zucchini) on the diagonal exposes more surface area so the food cooks more quickly and absorbs more flavor.

Matchstick or Julienne Cutting: Cut the ingredient into thin slices of the desired length. Stack the slices and cut down through the stacks lengthwise, to about the size of wooden matchstick pieces. For thicker sticks, start with thicker slices; for fine shreds, start with very thin slices.

Cubing, Dicing, Mincing: Generally, cubing means about ¾-inch cubes; dicing, ½- to ¼-inch cubes; and mincing, about ¹⁄₁₆-inch pieces. First cut the ingredient into matchstick pieces as above. Cut across the sticks to make cubes of the desired size. For finer mincing, go one step further: using the tip of the cleaver as a pivot, rock the blade in a back and forth motion, occasionally scooping the bits into a pile, until desired size is reached.

Crushing: To release the flavors of ingredients like garlic, ginger, or fermented black beans prior to mincing or adding to a marinade, place the ingredient on a cutting board and smack it with the broad side of the blade. Beans can also be crushed with the handle end of a cleaver.

Meat Cutting: For stir-frying, boneless meats — particularly beef — are always cut across the grain (at right angles to the direction of the fibers) into thin slices.

A heavy chopping cleaver, either Chinese or Western-style, is needed to cut through large bones (like cutting spareribs into shorter lengths or cutting poultry through the bones into cooking or serving pieces). Chop with one hard, straight downward motion.

Cooking Techniques

Stir-frying: This is the most common technique used in Chinese restaurant or home cooking. The process is simple, logical, and quick. First, a wok or wide frying pan is heated over a high temperature until hot. Seasonings like garlic and ginger are added to flavor the oil. Meat should be added next and tossed rapidly in the hot oil to seal in juices. (Meat is usually cooked before vegetables and removed; meat drippings will flavor the vegetables.)

Organization is essential in stir-frying. Have everything cut, measured, and marinated as needed before heating the wok. Meats and vegetables should be cut into uniform sizes to ensure even cooking. Vegetables are added according to their length of cooking time, with the toughest and most dense added first (eg. carrots, green pepper, onion, then snow peas, bean sprouts).

Meat is returned to the wok along with the cornstarch solution near the end of cooking. This sauce gently binds the ingredients and carries the seasonings.

Steaming: Cooking food over steaming water is one of the best ways to maintain the natural taste and nutritional value of fresh ingredients.

There are two methods of steaming, "open" and "closed." In the open method, food is placed directly on a heatproof dish or directly on the steamer rack. Bring the water to a boil before adding the food. Cover, and

14

steam for the specified time, adding additional water as needed. In closed steaming, also called double boiling, food is placed in a covered earthenware casserole which is placed in a larger pot and covered again. This technique usually takes several hours and gives an intensely flavored broth.

Blanching: This technique is mostly used for vegetables. Food is submerged in boiling water for a short time, removed, and immediately rinsed under cold water to stop further cooking. Blanching is used to pre-cook dense vegetables for stir-frying, to remove a metallic taste from canned vegetables like bamboo shoots, or to remove the skin from nuts. In restaurants, meats are sometimes "blanched" in hot oil to seal in their juices.

Smoking: Smoking is a technique used to add additional flavor to meats. Originally, Chinese chefs used huge ovens, but the method can be done in a wok. Combine smoking agents like black tea leaves, camphor chips, brown sugar, and rice; mix well and place on the bottom of a foil-lined wok. Set a rack in the wok and place pre-cooked meat on the rack. Cover the wok, turn up the heat, and in a few minutes the smoke will permeate the meat and impart a robust, smoky flavor. Chicken and duck are popular smoking items on a Chinese menu.

Roasting: In China, roasting is more a restaurant technique than one done in a home oven. In traditional Chinese ovens, marinated or sauce-coated meats hang on a hook and cook over a wood-burning fire. It is easy to approximate the method in a Western oven. Place the meat on a rack set in a foil-lined baking pan. Baste the meat with marinade or pan juices as it roasts and turn it occasionally.

Simmering: This is a technique of gently cooking food just below the boiling point in enough liquid to cover it. Broths, stews, and sauces are made this way. Foods cooked using this method are normally tender, juicy, and flavorful.

Braising: Braising is a two-step process. Meat is first browned to seal in juices, as in stir-frying. Then it is covered and simmered in a liquid until tender. The longer cooking time allows the flavors of the sauce to permeate the meat.

Red-cooking: When meats are simmered or braised in a liquid containing soy sauce and other seasonings, they are known as "red-cooked." Large pieces of meat or whole chickens may be browned first, then simmered in a liquid such as the Red-cooking Sauce on page 179.

Deep-frying: Deep-frying means the total submersion of food in hot oil. For safety, use a flat-bottomed wok, or set the wok in a ring stand to prevent it from tipping. Pour in oil to a depth of 2 to 2½ inches and heat to the specified temperature. Use a deep-frying thermometer and adjust the heat to maintain the proper temperature. If the oil is not hot enough, food cooks too slowly, absorbing oil, and the result is greasy. If it is too hot, the outside browns quickly, leaving the inside uncooked.

   Before adding the ingredients to the hot oil, pat them dry, then lightly dry-coat each piece with cornstarch or flour to absorb any extra moisture to prevent the oil from spattering. Slide the food, a few pieces at a time, into the hot oil; adding too much food at once lowers the temperature. Turn the pieces as they cook and lift them out with a slotted spoon to drain on paper towels.

Opposite: Chicken with Fragrant Fruit Sauce (page 129)

p. 20, top to bottom: Glazed Sesame Meatballs (page 26), Grilled Skewered Prawns (page 23), Baked Stuffed Mushrooms (page 25), Paper-wrapped Chicken (page 22) ▶

An assortment of fanciful Chinese vegetable garnishes *(see pages 180-181).*

19

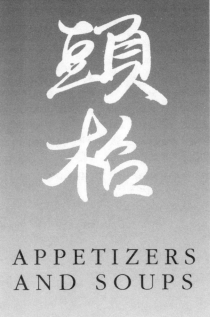

APPETIZERS AND SOUPS

In this chapter you will find an assortment of "little foods" — dishes to perk up your appetite at the beginning of a meal and set the stage for the delights to follow. But don't worry too much about classification; any of these foods can be served as part of a meal of several dishes served all at once. If you want to serve, say, Paper-wrapped Chicken (page 22) or Glazed Sesame Meatballs (page 26) at the same time as other dishes, feel free to do so.

These appetizers are also ideal for buffets and cocktail parties. Several can be made ahead of time, and others can be kept warm in a chafing dish. A few, like the Grilled Skewered Prawns on page 23, can even be served as a cook-it-yourself affair.

Soup is nearly always part of a traditional Chinese meal. Unlike Western soups, it is not served as a separate course, but is served and eaten alongside the other dishes. However, any of the soups in this chapter can be served Western style as a first course.

Also in this chapter are an assortment of the delicious little foods known as dim sum. If you don't live near a Cantonese tea house, you can still enjoy a brunch or lunch of these steamed, baked, and deep-fried tidbits with a pot of fragrant tea.

Paper-wrapped Chicken

In a Chinese restaurant, these little packages of fragrant marinated chicken would be deep-fried, but home cooks will find it easier to bake them in the oven. Baking parchment is available in well-stocked supermarkets and cookware shops; you can also use aluminum foil. (Photo, page 20)

Makes: 16 appetizers

Marinade
1	tablespoon Shao Hsing wine or dry sherry
1	tablespoon oyster-flavored sauce
2	teaspoons soy sauce
2	teaspoons sesame oil
1	teaspoon minced fresh ginger
¼	teaspoon cornstarch

■ ■ ■

1	whole chicken breast, skinned, boned, and cut into ½ x 2 x ¼-inch pieces
16	six-inch squares cooking parchment or foil
	Sesame oil
1	ounce Smithfield ham, cut into 1½-inch slivers
2	green onions (including tops), cut into 1½-inch slivers
⅓	cup sliced water chestnuts
¼	cup cilantro (Chinese parsley) leaves

Preparation

Combine marinade ingredients in a small bowl. Add chicken and stir to coat. Set aside for 30 minutes.

To wrap chicken, place a square of parchment paper on work surface with one point facing you. Brush lightly with sesame oil. Place 2 or 3 pieces of chicken in center of square. Top with a few slivers of ham and green onion, 1 slice of water chestnut, and a few cilantro leaves. Fold bottom corner over filling. Fold right and left corners in toward center, overlapping and enclosing filling. Fold filled part of packet in half. Slide top corner all the way down into space between layers of paper to seal packet. Repeat until all packets are made. If made ahead, cover and refrigerate for up to 4 hours.

Cooking

Preheat oven to 375°F. Place packets in a single layer in a shallow-rimmed baking pan. Bake in preheated oven for 15 minutes or until chicken is opaque (open a packet to test). To eat, untuck the flap with your fork or chopsticks and spread out the paper.

Tip: If you use foil as a wrapper, fold the filled square in half to make a triangle; double-fold open edges of triangle to seal.

Grilled Skewered Prawns

A simple hoisin marinade gives a slightly sweet glaze to succulent grilled prawns. You can also cook them under the broiler. For an informal party, let your guests grill their own skewers on a tabletop gas or electric grill, or use a small charcoal grill outdoors. (Photo, page 20)

Makes: About 16 appetizers

Marinade
¼   cup hoisin sauce
2   tablespoons soy sauce
2   tablespoons vegetable oil
1   tablespoon sesame oil
    Pinch of black pepper

■   ■   ■

1   pound medium-size raw shrimp, peeled and deveined
16   bamboo skewers
1   can (8 oz.) pineapple chunks, drained
1   red or green bell pepper, seeded and cut into 1-inch squares

Preparation

Combine marinade ingredients in a bowl. Add shrimp and stir to coat. Cover and refrigerate for 1 hour.

Soak bamboo skewers in water for 10 minutes.

Remove shrimp from marinade; reserve marinade. On each skewer, thread 1 shrimp, 1 pineapple chunk, 1 piece bell pepper, and 1 more shrimp.

Cooking

Place skewers on a well-oiled grill 2 to 3 inches above a solid bed of low-glowing coals. Cook, basting frequently with reserved marinade, for 3 minutes on each side or until shrimp feel firm and turn pink.

Tip: Because labeling varies from market to market, the most accurate way to judge a medium-size shrimp is by count. For this appetizer, look for 31 to 35 shrimp per pound.

Shrimp Toast

These crispy golden appetizers are a favorite all over southern China and Southeast Asia. The bread can be cut into any shape you like, such as triangles or diamonds. I like to use a round cookie cutter about 2 inches in diameter and curl up a half shrimp on top of the shrimp paste, with its tail pointing upward. (Photo, page 38)

Makes: 20 appetizers

10   **sandwich-size slices firm, day-old white bread**

Shrimp Paste
¼   **cup whole water chestnuts**
½   **pound medium-size raw shrimp, peeled and deveined**
1   **egg white**
2   **teaspoons cornstarch**
2   **teaspoons Shao Hsing wine or dry sherry**
½   **teaspoon minced fresh ginger**
½   **teaspoon salt**
⅛   **teaspoon white pepper**
1   **green onion (including top), minced**

    ■   ■   ■

10   **medium-size raw shrimp, peeled and deveined**
    Vegetable oil for deep-frying
    Fresh chives, chopped for garnish

Preparation

With a 2-inch cookie cutter, cut 2 circles from each bread slice; set aside.

Place water chestnuts in a food processor and process until coarsely chopped. Add remaining shrimp paste ingredients, except green onion. Process until mixture forms a chunky paste. Transfer to a bowl; stir in green onion.

Spread shrimp paste about ¼ inch thick on one side of each bread circle. Cut whole shrimp in half lengthwise. Curl one half shrimp on top of each circle of bread, pressing it firmly into shrimp paste.

Cooking

Set wok in a ring stand and add oil to a depth of about 2 inches. Place over medium-high heat until oil reaches 360°F. Add circles shrimp side down, a few at a time, and cook for 1 minute. Turn over and cook for 1 more minute or until golden brown. Lift out and drain on paper towels. Keep warm in a 200°F oven while cooking remaining shrimp toast. Sprinkle with chopped chives and serve immediately.

Tip: Use a deep-frying thermometer to gauge the temperature of the oil, or test the oil the Chinese way by standing a wooden chopstick on the bottom of the wok. When the oil bubbles briskly around the chopstick, it is hot enough for deep-frying.

Baked Stuffed Mushrooms

Chinese cooks love to stuff things — leafy vegetables, pasta, shrimp, even slices of bell pepper. Here, large mushroom caps are stuffed with a colorful mixture of rice, diced vegetables, black mushrooms, and shrimp. Try it for stuffing other vegetables, from artichoke bottoms to zucchini. (Photo, page 20)

Makes: 28 appetizers

2 dried black mushrooms

Sauce
¼   **cup chicken broth**
1   **tablespoon Shao Hsing wine or dry sherry**
1   **tablespoon soy sauce**
1   **teaspoon sesame oil**
1   **tablespoon cornstarch mixed with 2 tablespoons water**

■   ■   ■

2   **tablespoons vegetable oil**
1½   **teaspoons minced garlic**
2   **tablespoons finely diced zucchini**
2   **tablespoons finely diced carrot**
¼   **cup finely chopped, cooked shrimp**
1   **green onion (including top), minced**
1   **cup cooked medium-grain rice**
2   **eggs, lightly beaten**
½   **teaspoon salt**
¼   **teaspoon pepper**
28   **large fresh mushrooms (2-inch diameter), stems removed**
⅓   **cup chicken broth**

Preparation

Soak black mushrooms in warm water to cover for 30 minutes; drain. Cut off and discard stems and finely chop caps. Set aside.

Combine sauce ingredients in a small saucepan and set aside.

Cooking

Place a wok or wide frying pan over high heat until hot. Add oil, swirling to coat sides. Add garlic and cook, stirring, until fragrant, about 5 seconds. Add black mushrooms, zucchini, and carrot; stir-fry for 1 minute. Add shrimp, green onion, and rice; mix well. Stir in eggs, salt, and pepper; turn off heat and mix well.

Mound about 2 rounded teaspoons of filling into each mushroom cap and press firmly. Place mushrooms filling side up in a shallow-rimmed baking pan. If assembled ahead, cover and refrigerate for up to 8 hours. Just before baking, pour broth around mushrooms. Preheat oven to 350°F. Bake, uncovered, in preheated oven for 15 minutes.

With a slotted spatula, transfer mushrooms to a serving platter; cover loosely to keep warm. Pour pan drippings into sauce mixture. Stirring constantly, cook over medium-high heat until sauce boils and thickens slightly.

Tip: Do not substitute long-grain rice in this recipe. It lacks the sticky quality which is necessary to bind the filling together.

For an easy garnish, thinly slice a carrot, then use a garnish cutter to stamp out tiny butterflies as shown in the photograph. If you don't have a cutter, slice the carrot into thin slivers. Blanch the carrot garnish in boiling water for 10 seconds to intensify the color.

Glazed Sesame Meatballs

These small meatballs studded with pieces of ginger and jicama are equally at home in a Chinese meal or Western-style cocktail party buffet. They can be formed ahead of time and chilled or frozen until ready to cook, and they keep well in a chafing dish. (Photo, page 20)

Makes: 36 meatballs

Meatballs

1	pound lean ground pork
⅓	cup finely chopped jicama
¼	cup cornstarch
2	tablespoons hoisin sauce
2	tablespoons Shao Hsing wine or dry sherry
1	tablespoon minced fresh ginger
1	tablespoon soy sauce
1	tablespoon grated lemon peel
2	teaspoons sesame oil

Glazing Mixture

3	tablespoons lemon juice
2	tablespoons packed brown sugar

■   ■   ■

1	tablespoon vegetable oil
2	tablespoons toasted sesame seeds

Preparation

Combine meatball ingredients in a medium bowl. Shape into meatballs about 1 inch in diameter. Set aside. Combine glazing mixture ingredients in a small bowl and set aside.

Cooking

Place a pan with a nonstick finish over medium-high heat until hot. Add vegetable oil, swirling to coat surface. Add meatballs and cook for 6 minutes, turning occasionally, until browned on all sides and meat is no longer pink in center. Drain oil from pan. Pour glazing mixture over meatballs and cook over high heat for 2 minutes or until meatballs are nicely glazed. Transfer to a serving platter and sprinkle with sesame seeds.

Tip: Regular ground pork available in the supermarket contains too much fat. Ask your butcher to grind one pound of lean pork.

Green Onion Pancakes

Flat, pan-fried breads flavored with green onion are a popular accompaniment to soups and stews in northern China. This is an especially easy version, cooked like a pancake.

Makes: 8 pancakes

3	eggs
1	teaspoon sugar
1	teaspoon sesame oil
¾	teaspoon salt
¼	teaspoon white pepper
¾	cup water
1½	cups all-purpose flour
1	green onion (including top), thinly sliced
8	teaspoons vegetable oil

Preparation

Combine eggs, sugar, sesame oil, salt, pepper, and water in a bowl; whisk until evenly blended. Add flour; whisk until smooth. Stir in green onion.

Cooking

Place a wide frying pan with a nonstick finish over medium heat until hot. Add 1 teaspoon of the oil, swirling to coat surface. For each pancake, pour ⅓ cup batter into pan; spread batter to make a 5-inch circle. Cook for 4 minutes or until top of pancake is dry and bottom is golden brown; turn pancake to lightly brown other side. Remove from pan and keep warm while cooking remaining pancakes. Add 1 teaspoon oil to pan to cook each pancake.

Tip: For a savory appetizer, add 2 tablespoons minced Smithfield ham to the batter.

Seaweed Rice Rolls

The dried sheets of seaweed known in Japanese as *nori* are familiar to lovers of sushi, but they are also popular in coastal China. For an informal meal or picnic, lay out all the ingredients on a platter, and let everyone assemble his own rolls, adding his choice of fillings. (Photo, page 37)

Makes: 16 cones

Seasoned Rice

2　teaspoons soy sauce
2　teaspoons seasoned rice vinegar
1　teaspoon Chinese mustard
1　cup uncooked medium-grain rice

■　　■　　■

8　sheets toasted nori (paper-thin sheets of seaweed)

Fillings

1　Chinese sausage (about 2 oz.)
1　small avocado
3　tablespoons lemon juice
½　cucumber, seeded and cut into matchstick pieces
½　cup small cooked shrimp
　Cilantro (Chinese parsley) sprigs
2　dozen chives, cut into 2-inch pieces

■　　■　　■

　Soy sauce
　Wasabi (Japanese horseradish)
　Chinese mustard

Preparation

Combine soy sauce, seasoned rice vinegar, and mustard in a small bowl; whisk until evenly blended. Set aside. Cook rice as directed on page 46. Scoop rice into a shallow pan. Pour soy sauce mixture over rice. Stir until liquid is absorbed. Let stand to cool at room temperature. Spoon into a serving bowl. If made ahead, cover tightly and hold at room temperature for up to 4 hours.

Cut each sheet of nori in half crosswise. Stack on a plate or in a basket.

Preheat oven to 350°F. Place Chinese sausage in a heatproof dish. Bake in preheated oven for 15 minutes or until slightly crisp. Let cool, then cut into thin diagonal slices. Halve, pit, and peel avocado. Slice lengthwise into thin strips. Moisten each slice with lemon juice to prevent browning.

On a serving platter, separately arrange sausage, avocado, cucumber, shrimp, cilantro, and chives. Set soy sauce, wasabi, and Chinese mustard alongside.

To assemble each cone, lay one piece of nori on a flat surface. Place one heaping tablespoon of rice over one end of seaweed. Arrange choice of filling on top of rice and roll up to form a cone. Drizzle soy sauce or a mixture of soy and wasabi or soy and Chinese mustard into cone.

Tip: Each package of nori contains 10 sheets. You can buy it pre-toasted or toast it yourself by passing each sheet over a low gas flame or an electric burner set on low until the color brightens and the nori becomes crisp. Package leftover nori in an airtight container. It will keep indefinitely at room temperature.

Velvet Corn Soup

This soup is luxuriously rich in texture, but actually quite low in calories. Minced chicken or crabmeat are also traditional in place of the shrimp.

Makes: 6 to 8 servings

6   cups chicken broth
¼   pound medium-size shrimp, peeled, deveined, and coarsely chopped
½   cup diced cooked ham
¼   cup coarsely chopped water chestnuts
1   can (16¾ oz.) cream-style corn
2   teaspoons sesame oil
½   teaspoon salt
⅛   teaspoon white pepper
3   tablespoons cornstarch mixed with ⅓ cup water
2   egg whites, lightly beaten
1   green onion (including top), thinly sliced

Cooking

Bring broth to a boil in a 3-quart pot. Add shrimp, ham, water chestnuts, corn, sesame oil, salt, and pepper and return to a boil. Add cornstarch solution and cook, stirring, until soup boils and thickens slightly. Remove from heat and slowly drizzle in egg whites, stirring constantly. Sprinkle with green onion.

Basic Chicken Broth

A good chicken broth is the basis of most Chinese soups, and it is an important ingredient in many other dishes as well. Chinese broths are simpler than Western ones — just the essence of the chicken plus a little ginger and green onion to heighten the flavor. Save any chicken bones and trimmings in the freezer until you accumulate enough to make broth. The broth can also be frozen.

Makes: 1½ quarts

8   **cups water**
2½ **pounds raw chicken bones**
3   **green onions (including tops), cut in half**
8   **thin slices fresh ginger**
   Pinch of pepper
   Salt to taste

Cooking

In a large pot, heat water and chicken bones to boiling. Skim off any foam that forms on the top. Reduce heat, cover, and simmer for 1½ hours. Add green onions, ginger, pepper, and salt and simmer for 30 minutes. Strain broth, discarding bones and seasonings. Skim and discard fat from broth.

To Make Rich Chicken Broth:

To make a richer, deeper-flavored broth for soups, stews, and sauces, substitute chicken broth for the water in the above recipe. Another way is to add pork bones and ham trimmings to the chicken bones.

Tip: Regular or rich chicken broth will keep in the refrigerator for a week or more if brought to a boil every other day. Freeze for longer storage.

Chinese Vegetarian Broth

For times when you want to serve an entirely meatless meal, or just when you want a change from chicken-based soups, try this aromatic vegetarian version. Other vegetables can be added in small quantities; fresh or dried mushrooms are a particularly good addition. Avoid strongly flavored vegetables like broccoli, green peppers, or cabbage or they will dominate the broth.

Makes: 2 quarts

1 **tablespoon vegetable oil**
8 **thin slices fresh ginger**
3 **cloves garlic, crushed**
1 **large onion, cut into 1½-inch squares**
4 **green onions (including tops), cut into 2-inch pieces**
9 **cups water**
4 **carrots, cut into ½-inch thick slices**
2 **stalks celery, cut into 2-inch pieces**
2 **sprigs cilantro (Chinese parsley), optional**
2 **tablespoons soy sauce**
2 **teaspoons salt**
½ **pod star anise**
½ **teaspoon toasted Sichuan peppercorns**
½ **teaspoon white pepper**

Cooking

Heat oil in a large stockpot over medium-high heat. Add ginger, garlic, onion, and green onions and cook, stirring, for 2 minutes. Add remaining ingredients and bring to a boil. Reduce heat, cover, and simmer for 1½ hours. Strain broth, discarding vegetables and seasonings.

Tomato Egg Flower Soup

The "egg flowers" in the title are the delicate strands of beaten egg which are drizzled over the soup just before serving.

Makes: 4 to 6 servings

4   dried black mushrooms
6   cups chicken broth
1   tablespoon Shao Hsing wine
     or dry sherry
1   medium tomato, peeled,
     seeded, and diced
2   tablespoons cornstarch
     mixed with ¼ cup water
1   egg, lightly beaten
1   teaspoon sesame oil
     Salt to taste
¼   teaspoon white pepper
1   green onion (including top),
     thinly sliced

Preparation

Soak mushrooms in warm water to cover for 30 minutes; drain and reserve 1 cup liquid. Cut off and discard stems and dice caps. Set aside.

Cooking

In a 3-quart pot, bring broth, wine, reserved mushroom soaking liquid, and mushrooms to a boil. Cook for 3 minutes. Add tomato and cook for 1 minute. Add cornstarch solution and cook, stirring, until soup boils and thickens slightly. Remove from heat and slowly drizzle in egg, stirring constantly. Season with sesame oil, salt, and pepper. Sprinkle with green onion.

Tip: To peel tomato, blanch in boiling water for 30 seconds, then rinse in cold water before stripping off skin. Cut tomato in half crosswise. Gently squeeze each half to remove seeds before dicing.

Wonton Soup

Wontons are so easy to make, why not make a double recipe and store the extras in the freezer? With some chicken broth on hand, you can make this soup in a few minutes. Feel free to try other fillings; half pork and half shrimp is a good combination.

Makes: 6 to 8 servings

Filling Mixture
- ¼ pound lean ground pork
- 1 tablespoon finely chopped water chestnuts
- 1 green onion (including top), minced
- 1 egg white
- 1½ teaspoons soy sauce
- ½ teaspoon sesame oil
- ½ teaspoon cornstarch
- ⅛ teaspoon salt

■ ■ ■

- 25 wonton wrappers (about ½ lb.)
- 1 egg white, lightly beaten
- 6 cups chicken broth
- ¼ cup sliced water chestnuts
- ¼ cup sliced bamboo shoots
- ½ teaspoon sesame oil
- Pinch of white pepper
- Thinly sliced green onion for garnish

Preparation

Combine filling ingredients in a small bowl and mix well.

To fill each wonton, place 1 heaping teaspoon of filling in center of a wonton wrapper; keep remaining wrappers covered to prevent drying. Brush edges of wrapper lightly with egg white. Fold in half over filling to form a triangle; press edges firmly to seal. Place filled wonton on a plate and cover with a damp cloth while filling remaining wrappers.

Cooking

In a large pot of boiling water, cook wontons for 2 minutes or until filling is no longer pink. Drain, then place in a bowl of cold water to prevent wontons from sticking together.

Bring broth to a boil in a large saucepan. Add water chestnuts, bamboo shoots, sesame oil, and white pepper and cook for 1 minute.

To serve, drain wontons, then add to hot broth. Garnish with green onion.

Tip: To freeze uncooked wontons, place on a baking sheet and freeze until firm. Transfer to a plastic bag and return to freezer. Cook frozen wontons for 4 minutes, then combine with broth.

Ginseng Chicken Soup

Whether or not you believe that ginseng has life-giving or aphrodisiac powers, it gives a unique flavor to this soup. Cooking the soup in a heatproof bowl placed inside a larger cooking pot is a classic Chinese technique for making the clearest, most delicately flavored broth. (Photo, page 140)

Makes: 2 servings

4	**chicken breast halves, skinned and boned**
3	**cups water**
4	**pieces (about 1 oz.) ginseng**
1	**medium-size ling chi, sliced (optional)**
	Salt to taste

Preparation

Trim excess fat from chicken breasts. Blanch chicken in boiling water for 1 minute; drain. Transfer all ingredients to an earthenware pot. Cover with lid and set aside.

Cooking

In a deep 8-quart stockpot, invert a custard cup or similar-size heatproof bowl. Pour water into stockpot until it reaches halfway up the side of the cup. Place covered earthenware pot on top of cup. Cover stockpot and bring water to a boil. Cook over medium-high heat for 4 hours or until ginseng flavor is extracted. Add additional water to stockpot as needed.

Tip: To provide the maximum heat needed to keep the soup simmering, keep the water in the stockpot at a vigorous boil.

Ling chi, a highly prized mushroom from the mountains of China, is believed to have restorative powers that contribute to longevity. It is sold in Chinese herbal shops. If you buy one, ask the shopkeeper to thinly slice the cap. It looks like a petrified mushroom and is very difficult to slice with an ordinary knife.

Sizzling Rice Hot and Sour Soup

Hot and Sour Soup can be a complicated affair, full of assorted dried fungus and other ingredients. This is a simpler version, designed to go with sizzling rice crusts.

Makes: 4 to 6 servings

4	dried black mushrooms
5	cups chicken broth
1	chicken breast half, skinned, boned, and cut into matchstick pieces
¼	cup slivered bamboo shoots
½	cup rice vinegar
2	tablespoons soy sauce
1	green onion (including top), cut into 2-inch slivers
1	teaspoon finely chopped cilantro (Chinese parsley)
1	teaspoon hot pepper sauce
½	teaspoon salt
½	teaspoon white pepper
3	tablespoons cornstarch mixed with ¼ cup water
1	egg, lightly beaten
	Vegetable oil for deep-frying
8	two-inch square rice crusts

Preparation

Soak mushrooms in warm water to cover for 30 minutes; drain. Cut off and discard stems and thinly slice caps. Set aside.

Cooking

Bring broth to a boil over medium-high heat in a large pot. Add chicken and cook, stirring occasionally, for 3 minutes. Stir in mushrooms, bamboo shoots, vinegar, soy sauce, green onion, cilantro, hot pepper sauce, salt, and white pepper. Return to a boil. Add cornstarch solution and cook, stirring, until soup thickens slightly. Remove pot from heat and slowly drizzle in egg, stirring constantly. Keep warm while preparing rice crusts.

Set wok in a ring stand and add oil to a depth of about 2 inches. Over high heat, bring oil to 375°F. Add rice crusts, half at a time, and cook, turning constantly, for 15 seconds or until puffed. Lift out and drain on paper towels. Cook remaining rice crusts. Pour hot soup into a warmed serving bowl and carry to the table. Bring hot fried rice crusts to the table and carefully slide into the soup.

Tip: Look for rice crusts in Chinese markets. To make your own rice crusts, see page 46.

Triple Mushroom Soup

This European-style creamy mushroom purée gets a Chinese accent from fresh ginger and cilantro. More varieties of mushrooms are coming on the market all the time, so try this soup with whatever mushrooms are available. (Photo, page 39)

Makes: 4 to 6 servings

8   dried black mushrooms
3   tablespoons butter or
     margarine
1   small onion, finely chopped
¼   pound fresh mushrooms,
     sliced
1   can (15 oz.) straw
     mushrooms, drained
1   teaspoon minced fresh
     ginger
3   tablespoons all-purpose flour
3¼   cups half-and-half
3   cilantro (Chinese parsley)
     sprigs
½   teaspoon salt
½   teaspoon sesame oil
⅛   teaspoon white pepper
     Fresh oyster mushrooms or
     enoki mushrooms for
     garnish
2   green onions (including
     tops), cut into 2-inch slivers
     for garnish
     Cilantro (Chinese parsley)
     leaves for garnish

Preparation

Soak black mushrooms in warm water to cover for 30 minutes; drain. Cut off and discard stems and thinly slice caps. Set aside.

Cooking

Melt butter in a 3-quart pan over medium heat. Add onion and cook for 2 minutes or until soft. Add black mushrooms, fresh mushrooms, straw mushrooms, and ginger and cook for 3 minutes or until mushrooms are soft and pan juices have evaporated. Stir in flour and cook for 1 minute. Stir in half-and-half and bring to a boil, stirring constantly.

Place soup and cilantro sprigs in a blender or food processor. Process mixture until smooth. Add salt, sesame oil, and pepper. Return soup to pan and reheat without boiling. Ladle soup into bowls. Garnish each serving with oyster mushrooms or enoki mushrooms, green onion slivers, and cilantro leaves.

Tip: Canned straw mushrooms come peeled and unpeeled. The peeled ones are the most tender and for general cooking purposes, they are the most decorative — they look like miniature umbrellas that are halfway open.

Seaweed Rice Rolls (page 28) ▶

Shrimp Toast *(page 24)*

Triple Mushroom Soup (page 36)

Quail Egg Siu Mai

Western cooks have recently "discovered" quail eggs, something we Chinese have been using as food for centuries. I like to use a whole cooked quail egg as part of the stuffing for *siu mai*, the small, open-topped steamed dumplings that are so popular for dim sum. (Photo, opposite page)

Makes: About 30 dumplings

Filling

¼   **pound lean ground pork**

¼   **pound medium-size shrimp, peeled, deveined, and coarsely chopped**

2   **tablespoons coarsely chopped bamboo shoots**

1   **tablespoon soy sauce**

1   **tablespoon Shao Hsing wine or dry sherry**

1   **tablespoon oyster-flavored sauce**

1   **teaspoon cornstarch**

1   **teaspoon sugar**

1   **teaspoon sesame oil**

¼   **teaspoon white pepper**

■   ■   ■

30   **wonton or siu mai wrappers (approx.)**

1   **can (15 oz.) quail eggs, drained**

  Soy sauce

  Chinese mustard

Preparation

Combine filling ingredients in a bowl and mix well. Set aside for 30 minutes.

If using wonton wrappers, trim edges to form circles. To fill each dumpling, place one quail egg in center of wrapper; keep remaining wrappers covered to prevent drying. Place 1 heaping teaspoon of filling on top of egg. Use fingers to gather up and pleat the wrapper around the filling to form an open-topped pouch. Carefully squeeze the middle to give it a waist. Cover with a damp cloth while filling remaining wrappers.

Cooking

Place steaming rack in a wok. Pour water to just below level of rack and bring to a boil. Arrange dumplings, meat side down, without crowding, on a lightly greased 9-inch glass pie dish or other heatproof dish and set on rack. Cover and steam, adding additional water if necessary, for 12 minutes or until meat is no longer pink in center. Serve with soy sauce or Chinese mustard for dipping, if desired.

Tip: If you can find fresh quail eggs, cook them in simmering water for 5 minutes, rinse in cold water, and peel them for this recipe; otherwise, use the precooked ones available in cans.

It may be necessary to steam the dumplings in batches; use stacking bamboo steamers or cook one batch after another.

◀   *Dim sum, clockwise from top: Quail Egg Siu Mai, Juicy Steamed Buns and baked variation (page 42), Golden Meat Turnovers (page 43), Egg Custard Tart (page 44)*

Juicy Steamed Buns

Steamed buns, puffy balls of tender dough enclosing a savory pork filling, are among the most popular dim sum dishes. These buns can also be baked pleated side down on a lightly greased baking sheet for 20 minutes at 350°F. Brush the tops with a thin egg wash before baking for a golden brown top. (Photo, page 40)

Makes: 24 buns

Filling
½ teaspoon unflavored gelatin
¼ cup chicken broth
½ pound lean ground pork
1 green onion (including top), thinly sliced
1 egg, lightly beaten
2 tablespoons soy sauce
1 tablespoon sesame oil
2 teaspoons Shao Hsing wine or dry sherry
1 teaspoon minced garlic
1 teaspoon sugar
1 teaspoon cornstarch

Dough
1 package (¼ oz.) active dry yeast
½ cup warm water (110°F)
2 cups all-purpose flour
2 tablespoons sugar
1 tablespoon shortening, melted and cooled

■   ■   ■

Chinese (napa) cabbage leaves for steaming

Preparation

In a small pan, stir together gelatin and chicken broth; let stand for 5 minutes or until gelatin has softened. Bring just to a boil, stirring constantly. Let mixture cool, then refrigerate until firm. Combine remaining filling ingredients in a medium bowl. Mash gelatin mixture with a fork. Add to filling, mix well, and refrigerate.

In a large bowl, dissolve yeast in water. Let stand at room temperature for 10 minutes or until frothy. Gradually mix in flour, sugar, and shortening. Add 1 or 2 tablespoons more water if dough does not hold together.

On a lightly floured surface, knead dough for 5 minutes or until smooth and elastic. Shape into a ball and place in a lightly greased bowl; turn dough over to grease top. Cover with a damp cloth and let rise in a warm area for about 1 hour or until doubled. Punch down dough and shape into a ball. Cover with a damp cloth and let rest for 10 to 15 minutes.

On a lightly floured surface, roll dough into a 12-inch-long cylinder. Cut cylinder in half, then cut each half crosswise into 12 pieces. Shape each piece into a ball.

To shape each bun, flatten one ball with a rolling pin to make a 3- to 3½-inch circle; keep remaining dough covered to prevent drying. Place 1 heaping teaspoon of filling in center of circle. Gather edges of circle over filling; close top by pleating, pinching, and twisting edges together. Place buns on a baking sheet at least 2 inches apart. Cover with a damp cloth and let rise in a warm place for 15 minutes or until light and puffy.

Cooking

Line the bottom of two bamboo steamers with cabbage leaves and arrange buns, without crowding, on leaves. Pour 2 inches of water into a wok and bring to a boil. Stack steamers in wok. Cover and steam for 10 minutes or until tops of buns are glazed and smooth. Serve warm.

Golden Meat-filled Turnovers

A good dim sum menu should include foods cooked by a variety of methods. Besides steamed and baked dishes, you might want to include at least one deep-fried item, such as these crisp little crescents of glutinous rice flour dough with a pork, dried shrimp, and mushroom filling. (Photo, page 40)

Makes: 32 turnovers

Turnover Dough
⅔ cup wheat starch
3 tablespoons lard, softened
½ cup boiling water
3 tablespoons packed brown sugar
½ teaspoon salt
2 cups glutinous rice flour
¾ cup cool water

Filling
10 small dried black mushrooms
¼ cup dried shrimp
2 tablespoons soy sauce
1 tablespoon Shao Hsing wine or dry sherry
¼ teaspoon white pepper
1 tablespoon cornstarch
2 tablespoons vegetable oil
¾ pound boneless lean pork, finely chopped
3 green onions (including tops), thinly sliced
¼ cup chopped water chestnuts

■ ■ ■

Vegetable oil for deep-frying

Preparation

Place wheat starch in a large bowl and mix with lard. Make a well in the center. Bring water to a rolling boil. Immediately add to wheat starch; mix well. Stir in brown sugar and salt. Add glutinous rice flour and cool water; mix well. On a lightly floured surface, knead dough for 5 minutes or until smooth and elastic. Shape dough into a 1-inch-thick patty. Wrap with plastic wrap and refrigerate for 2 hours.

Soak mushrooms and shrimp separately in warm water to cover for 30 minutes; drain. Cut off and discard mushroom stems and coarsely chop caps. Set mushrooms and shrimp aside. In a bowl, combine soy sauce, wine, pepper, and cornstarch; set aside.

Place a wok or wide frying pan over medium-high heat until hot. Add oil, swirling to coat sides. Add pork and stir-fry for 1 minute. Add mushrooms and shrimp and cook for 1 minute. Add green onions and water chestnuts and cook for 1 minute. Stir in soy sauce mixture and cook for 1 minute. Transfer to a plate and let cool.

Dust work surface with glutinous rice flour. Roll dough into two 16-inch-long cylinders. Cut each cylinder into 16 pieces. Shape each piece into a ball. Using your fingers, press one ball into a 4-inch circle. Place 2 teaspoons of filling in center of circle. Fold in half to form a half moon shape. Pinch edges to seal. Place filled turnover on a plate and cover with a damp cloth while filling remaining turnovers.

Cooking

Set wok in a ring stand and add oil to a depth of about 2 inches. Place over medium-high heat until oil reaches 360°F. Cook turnovers a few at a time for 4 minutes or until golden brown. Lift out and drain on paper towels. Cook remaining turnovers. Serve warm.

Egg Custard Tarts

These delicate lemon-flavored tarts are equally at home as part of a dim sum meal or an English-style afternoon tea. The dough, a sort of simplified puff pastry, can be made up to 2 days ahead of time and stored in the refrigerator until ready for the final rolling. (Photo, page 40)

Makes: 14 tarts

Pastry Dough
½ cup lard, chilled and diced
¼ cup unsalted butter, chilled and diced
1 egg
1¾ cups all-purpose flour
2 tablespoons ice water
1 teaspoon vanilla extract

Filling
⅔ cup sugar
⅔ cup boiling water
⅓ cup evaporated milk
4 eggs, lightly beaten
½ teaspoon vanilla extract

Preparation

Place chilled lard, butter, and egg in a food processor. Process mixture for 4 seconds. Add flour and process until lumps are the size of peas. Add water and vanilla and process a few seconds longer. (Do not overprocess.) Mixture should be crumbly. Press crumbs together, shape into a patty 1 inch thick, and wrap with plastic wrap. Chill for 45 minutes.

On a lightly floured surface, roll out dough ¼ inch thick to form a long rectangle. If dough becomes soft and sticky during the rolling and folding process, return dough to refrigerator and chill until firm. Fold the rectangle of dough into thirds, as if folding a letter, then turn dough 90 degrees. Roll out again into a rectangle ¼ inch thick and fold into thirds. Cover with plastic wrap. Let dough rest in refrigerator for 20 minutes.

Meanwhile, prepare filling. In a large bowl, dissolve sugar in boiling water; let cool to room temperature. Whisk in evaporated milk and eggs. Stir in vanilla and refrigerate until ready to use. Remove chilled dough from refrigerator and place on a lightly floured surface. Roll out dough into a large rectangle about ¼ inch thick. Cut out 14 circles with a 4-inch round cutter. Center each pastry circle in a 2½-inch tart tin. Lightly press dough into bottom and sides of tin; trim edges. Chill for 1 hour or overnight.

Cooking

Preheat oven to 300°F. Pour filling into pastry-lined tins to within ¼ inch of the top. Place filled tins on a cookie sheet; bake in preheated oven for 35 minutes or until a knife inserted in center comes out clean. Cool slightly. Carefully turn tins upside down, gently tapping to release crust. Cool, custard side up, on a wire rack. Serve warm or at room temperature.

RICE AND
NOODLES

···

Grains are by far the most important foods in China, as in most parts of the world. In central and southern China, rice is the "staff of life," and after all my years of living in the West, I still feel a meal is incomplete without rice in some form. In the cooler, drier north, wheat is more common, whether it is made into breads or noodles.

All the other recipes in this book, whether for vegetables, meats, poultry, or seafood, are intended to accompany rice or noodles to make a meal. In fact, some of the recipes in this chapter combine rice or noodles and other foods in one-dish meals, such as Chinese Paella (page 51) or Stone Soup with Rice Noodles (page 63).

Rice comes in several varieties, including long, medium, and short grains, glutinous and non-glutinous types. Each has its own cooking qualities, and these are discussed in the glossary and on the next page. The glossary also covers the many varieties of noodles used in Chinese cooking. They may be made of wheat flour and water, flour and egg, rice flour, or bean starch; again, each has its particular uses.

How to Cook Perfect Rice

The following recipe is the classic Chinese way to cook rice. It makes a slightly sticky-grained rice just like you would find in a Chinese restaurant. If you prefer rice where the grains are more separate, add 1 cup rice to 1½ cups boiling water and simmer, covered, for 15 to 20 minutes.

Makes: About 3 cups

1   cup uncooked long-grain rice
1½ cups water

Cooking

Place rice and water in a medium saucepan and bring to a boil over medium-high heat. Boil, uncovered, for 10 minutes or until water evaporates and crater-like holes appear. Reduce heat to low; cover and simmer for 15 minutes or until rice is tender. Remove from heat and let stand, covered, for 5 minutes. Fluff with fork.

To Make Rice Crusts:

Combine 1 cup medium- or short-grain rice and 1 cup water in a medium saucepan. Cover and bring to a boil over high heat. Reduce heat to low and simmer for 25 minutes. Turn off heat and let stand for 5 minutes. Spread cooked rice in a ¼-inch-thick layer in a greased, shallow baking pan. Cut into 1½- to 2-inch squares with a wet knife. Bake in a 350°F oven for 50 minutes or until rice squares are firm and dry. Store rice crusts in an airtight container at room temperature for up to 6 months.

Rice in a Lotus Leaf

This is a very traditional rice dish, typically served in a Cantonese dim sum tea lunch or during Chinese New Year. Cooked rice is combined with assorted savory ingredients, wrapped in lotus leaves, and steamed, giving it a delicately fragrant scent and a moister and softer texture than everyday rice. This can also be prepared with glutinous rice. (Photo, page 58)

Makes: 4 to 6 servings

¼ **cup dried shrimp**
4 **dried black mushrooms**
2 **large dried lotus leaves**
1 **tablespoon vegetable oil**
2 **shallots, chopped**
1 **Chinese sausage (about 2 oz.), cut diagonally into ⅛-inch-thick slices**
½ **cup diced cooked ham**
¼ **cup diced celery**
1 **teaspoon chopped cilantro (Chinese parsley)**
2 **tablespoons soy sauce**
1 **tablespoon sesame oil**
3 **cups cooked medium-grain rice**

Preparation

Soak dried shrimp in warm water to cover for 30 minutes; drain and coarsely chop. Set aside.

Soak mushrooms in warm water to cover for 30 minutes; drain. Cut off and discard stems and thinly slice caps. Set aside.

Cooking

Bring water to a boil in a large pan. Plunge lotus leaves into boiling water and cook for 2 minutes or until softened; drain well. Set aside.

Place a wok or wide frying pan over high heat until hot. Add vegetable oil, swirling to coat sides. Add shallots, sausage, and shrimp and stir-fry for 1 minute. Add ham, celery, cilantro, and mushrooms and stir-fry for 1 minute. Stir in soy sauce and sesame oil. Stir in rice, separating grains with the back of a spoon; mix well. Remove from heat. Spread one lotus leaf on work surface. Cover with second leaf. Place rice mixture in center of lotus leaves. Fold edges of leaves over rice so rice is completely covered. Place steaming rack in a wok. Pour water to just below level of rack and bring to a boil. Place lotus leaf packet on a heatproof dish and set dish on rack. Cover and steam, adding additional water if neccessary, for 30 minutes.

Tip: This may be cooked ahead of time. To reheat, steam until hot or reheat in the microwave.

Lotus leaves are prized as a wrapper because they contribute both aroma and flavor. Look for packages of dried leaves in Oriental markets. They will keep indefinitely in a cool, dry place. If you cannot find large leaves, divide rice mixture in half and make two smaller packets. Parchment paper or foil may be used in place of lotus leaves.

Rice Congee

When rice is cooked with a lot of liquid, the result is congee. This bland-tasting porridge is popular for breakfast and late-night snacks. It is almost always served with a variety of meats, seafood, and condiments. In this recipe, a variety of fresh seafood is used. If you live near a Chinatown, you might find bakeries selling long, crisp, cylindrical Chinese doughnuts, another traditional accompaniment.

Makes: 6 to 8 servings

¼   **pound squid**

Marinade
1   **tablespoon Shao Hsing wine or dry sherry**
2   **teaspoons cornstarch**
¼   **teaspoon salt**
     Pinch of white pepper
          ■   ■   ■
¼   **pound medium-size raw shrimp, peeled and deveined**
¼   **pound sea scallops, cut in half horizontally**
1¼   **cups uncooked long-grain rice**
4   **thin slices fresh ginger**
12   **cups chicken broth**
1   **teaspoon sesame oil**

Toppings (optional)
     Chopped cilantro (Chinese parsley)
     Thinly sliced green onion
     Deep-fried wonton strips
     Deep-fried dried bean thread noodles
     Roasted whole peanuts

Preparation

To clean squid, separate head and tentacles from body. Cut off tentacles just above eyes, then remove and discard hard beak at center of tentacles. Rinse tentacles and set aside. Discard remainder of head. Pull out still pen from body. Slit body open and rinse thoroughly. Peel off speckled membrane and rinse again. Lightly score inside of body in a small crisscross pattern. Cut body into 1½- by 2-inch pieces.

Combine marinade ingredients in a medium bowl. Add squid, shrimp, and scallops and stir to coat. Refrigerate until ready to use.

Cooking

Combine rice, ginger, and broth in a large pot and bring to a boil. Cover and simmer, stirring occasionally, for 1½ hours or until rice becomes very soft and creamy. Remove ginger slices. Add squid, shrimp, and scallops and simmer, stirring occasionally, for 10 minutes. Stir in sesame oil.

To serve, ladle congee into individual soup bowls and offer a variety of toppings.

Tomato Beef Fried Rice

Like *chow mein*, fried rice is a whole genre of cooking, a versatile technique that can be adapted to most stir-fried dishes. A wok is traditional, but I find a nonstick frying pan works even better, and is much easier to clean.

Makes: 4 to 6 servings

Sauce

3	tablespoons ketchup
2	tablespoons soy sauce
2	teaspoons sesame oil
½	teaspoon salt

■ ■ ■

2	tablespoons vegetable oil
½	pound lean ground beef
1	small onion, chopped
2	green onions (including tops), thinly sliced
4	cups cooked long-grain rice
1	medium tomato, peeled, seeded, and chopped
½	cup frozen peas, thawed
2	eggs, lightly beaten

Preparation

Combine sauce ingredients in a small bowl and set aside.

Cooking

Place a wide frying pan with a nonstick finish over high heat until hot. Add oil, swirling to coat surface. Add beef and stir-fry for 1 minute. Add onion and green onions and stir-fry for 2 minutes. Reduce heat to medium and stir in rice, separating grains with the back of a spoon. Add tomato, peas, and eggs and cook, stirring constantly, for 1 minute. Add sauce and cook, stirring, until heated through.

Jambalaya à la Chinoise

I understand there are a lot of Chinese living in southern Louisiana. I wonder if this is how they would cook a jambalaya? My thanks to chef T.J. Robinson, who shared her recipe from her Gingerbread House Restaurant in Oakland, California. I added some Chinese five-spice and Chinese sausage to give it an Oriental touch.

Makes: 4 to 6 servings

¼ **cup dried shrimp**

T.J.'s Secret Spice Mix
½ **teaspoon cayenne pepper**
½ **teaspoon salt**
½ **teaspoon crushed red pepper**
¼ **teaspoon black pepper**
¼ **teaspoon thyme**
¼ **teaspoon sage**
¼ **teaspoon Chinese five-spice**
⅛ **teaspoon white pepper**
⅛ **teaspoon paprika**
2 **bay leaves**

■   ■   ■

2 **tablespoons vegetable oil**
4 **teaspoons all-purpose flour**
1 **Chinese sausage (about 2 oz.), thinly sliced**
1 **Andouille sausage, sliced**
2 **teaspoons minced garlic**
½ **onion, finely chopped**
3 **green onions (including tops), thinly sliced**
1 **green bell pepper, diced**
½ **red bell pepper, diced**
½ **cup diced celery**
1 **cup uncooked long-grain rice**
1½ **cups chicken broth**
½ **pound medium-size raw shrimp, peeled (leave tail intact) and deveined**
   Cilantro (Chinese parsley) sprigs for garnish

Preparation

Soak dried shrimp in warm water to cover for 30 minutes; drain and set aside. Combine spice mix ingredients in a small bowl and set aside.

Cooking

Place a wok or wide frying pan over medium-high heat until hot. Add oil, swirling to coat sides. Add flour and stir to blend well. Add Chinese and Andouille sausages and dried shrimp and cook, stirring, for 2 minutes. Add garlic, onion, green onions, green and red bell peppers, and celery and stir-fry for 30 seconds. Add spice mix and cook, stirring, for 30 seconds. Add rice and stir for 1 minute. Pour in broth, cover, and cook over medium heat for 8 minutes. Reduce heat to medium-low and cook for 15 minutes. Lay shrimp on top of rice; cover and cook for 5 minutes longer or until shrimp feel firm and turn pink and rice is tender to bite. Garnish with cilantro sprigs.

Tip: Do not stir rice during cooking.

Andouille (pronounced on-do-ee) is a Cajun-style smoked pork sausage. If you cannot find it, substitute kielbasa.

Chinese Paella

Paella, Spain's most famous dish, is undoubtedly one of the world's great rice dishes. The first time I saw a traditional Spanish paella pan, I thought it was a particularly shallow flat-bottomed wok. That got me thinking about how a Chinese cook would prepare the same dish. The result is this East-West hybrid, cooked in a wok. An electric wok works especially well for this dish. (Photo, page 57)

Makes: 6 servings

8   dried black mushrooms
12   medium-size raw shrimp
6   chicken drumsticks or 12 chicken wing drumettes
     Salt and pepper to taste
¼   teaspoon Chinese five-spice
12   live mussels, scrubbed, beards removed; or 12 live small hard-shell clams, scrubbed
½   cup water
3¾   cups (approx.) chicken broth
2   tablespoons vegetable oil
2   teaspoons minced garlic
2   teaspoons minced fresh ginger
1   large onion, chopped
1   red bell pepper, seeded and chopped
½   teaspoon turmeric
2   cups uncooked long-grain rice
2   Chinese sausages (about 2 oz. each), cut into ¼-inch diagonal slices
1   small whole bamboo shoot, cut lengthwise into thin wedges
12   snow peas, ends and strings removed
¼   cup chopped cilantro (Chinese parsley)

Preparation

Soak mushrooms in warm water to cover for 30 minutes; drain. Cut off and discard stems and slice caps in half. Set aside.

Remove shrimp legs, leaving shells and tails intact. Cut along backs of shrimp with scissors; rinse out sand veins. Sprinkle chicken with salt, pepper, and five-spice. Set aside.

Cooking

Bring mussels or clams and water to a boil in a 2-quart pan. Cover, reduce heat to low, and cook for 5 minutes or until shells open. Lift out mussels and set aside; pour liquid into a 4-cup measuring cup. Add enough chicken broth to make 4 cups total liquid.

Place a wok over high heat until hot. Add oil, swirling to coat sides. Add garlic and ginger and cook, stirring, until fragrant, about 5 seconds. Add chicken and cook, turning as needed, for 10 minutes or until well browned on all sides. Add 2 tablespoons chicken broth. Cover and cook for 5 minutes. Remove chicken and set aside. Add onion and cook for 1 minute. Add bell pepper and turmeric; cook for 1 minute. Add rice, sausages, and the reserved 4 cups chicken broth. Bring to a boil, and cook, uncovered, for 10 minutes or until broth evaporates and crater-like holes appear. Arrange chicken, Chinese sausages, bamboo shoot, and mushrooms over rice. Reduce heat, cover, and simmer for 20 minutes. Push shrimp into top of rice and scatter snow peas on top. Cover and cook for 5 minutes. Push mussels into rice. Cover and cook for 5 more minutes or until rice is tender to bite. Sprinkle with cilantro before serving.

Beijing Pizza

What is this dish doing in the Rice and Noodles chapter? Well, in the Chinese scheme of things, bread is *fan*, the rice- or wheat-based foods that are the "staff of life." If the Chinese had invented pizza, this is probably what it would have tasted like.

Makes: Two 12-inch pizzas

Dough

¼	cup warm water (110°F.)
1	package (¼ oz.) active dry yeast
3	cups all-purpose flour
1	teaspoon salt
¾	cup cold water
2	tablespoons vegetable oil
1	tablespoon honey

Sauce

½	cup hoisin sauce
¼	cup tomato paste
2	teaspoons minced garlic
2	green onions (including tops), thinly sliced

■ ■ ■

Toppings

8	dried black mushrooms
3	Chinese sausages (about 2 oz. each)
2	cups sliced fresh mushrooms
1	can (15 oz.) peeled straw mushrooms, drained and cut in half
2	tablespoons chopped cilantro (Chinese parsley)
2	cups (8 oz.) shredded mozzarella cheese

■ ■ ■

Cilantro (Chinese parsley) sprigs for garnish

Preparation

Pour warm water into a small bowl. Sprinkle yeast over water and stir until dissolved. Let stand for 10 minutes or until small bubbles form. Place flour and salt in a food processor; process for 10 seconds. In a 1-cup glass measure, combine cold water, oil, and honey. With processor running, pour honey mixture down feed tube. With motor still running, pour dissolved yeast down feed tube. Process until mixture forms a ball. On a lightly floured surface, knead dough for 5 minutes or until smooth and elastic. Place dough in a lightly greased bowl; turn to coat. Cover bowl with a dry cloth. Let rise in a warm area for 1 hour or until doubled in bulk.

To prepare sauce, combine hoisin sauce, tomato paste, and garlic in a bowl. Whisk until well blended. Set aside. Soak black mushrooms in warm water to cover for 30 minutes; drain. Cut off and discard stems and thinly slice caps. Set aside. In a small saucepan, cover sausages with water and bring to a boil; drain. Cut into ⅛-inch-thick diagonal slices.

Punch dough down and knead in green onions. Divide dough in half. Flatten each half and roll out to form a 12-inch circle. If green onions begin to come out, press back into dough. Transfer each circle to a greased 12-inch pizza pan; pat dough firmly into pan edge.

To assemble each pizza, spread half of sauce over dough. Arrange half of toppings, except cheese, over sauce. Sprinkle evenly with cheese.

Cooking

Preheat oven to 450°F. Bake pizza in lower third of oven for 15 minutes or until cheese melts and bottom of crust is browned. If baking two pizzas at once, switch pans halfway through baking. Garnish each pizza with cilantro.

Pasta with Spicy Meat Sauce

All of the ingredients in this sauce keep well, making it an ideal dish for a busy weeknight. Pick up some ground meat on the way home (or pull some out of the freezer in the morning to thaw in the refrigerator), and you can whip up a hot, tasty pasta dish in a quarter of an hour.

Makes: 6 servings

Sauce

½   cup tomato sauce
½   cup beef broth
1   tablespoon soy sauce
1   tablespoon Worcestershire sauce
2   teaspoons curry powder
2   teaspoons chili paste
1   teaspoon sugar

■   ■   ■

1   package (about 1 lb.) fresh egg noodles
2   teaspoons sesame oil
1   tablespoon vegetable oil
2   teaspoons minced garlic
1   teaspoon minced fresh ginger
¾   pound lean ground pork or ground beef
½   small onion, coarsely chopped
2   teaspoons cornstarch mixed with 4 teaspoons water
2   green onions (including tops), thinly sliced for garnish

Preparation

Combine sauce ingredients in a medium bowl and set aside.

Cooking

In a large pot of boiling water, cook noodles according to package directions until tender but firm to the bite. Drain well. Toss noodles with sesame oil. Transfer to a serving bowl and set aside.

Place a wok or wide frying pan over high heat until hot. Add vegetable oil, swirling to coat sides. Add garlic, ginger, pork, and onion and stir-fry for 3 minutes or until meat is browned and crumbly. Add sauce and bring to a boil. Reduce heat and simmer for 3 minutes. Add cornstarch solution and cook, stirring, until sauce boils and thickens. Pour sauce over noodles. Garnish with green onions.

Shanghai Chow Mein

Chow mein — literally "pan-fried noodles" — can take different forms in Chinese cooking. In this version, also known as *lo mein* (tossed noodles), cooked noodles are stir-fried along with the meat and vegetables. Just about any stir-fried dish can be prepared this way, making it a handy way to turn a single dish into a meal. (Photo, page 60)

Makes: 6 servings

Marinade
1   tablespoon soy sauce
2   teaspoons cornstarch

■   ■   ■

2   chicken breast halves, skinned, boned, and thinly sliced
1   package (about 1 lb.) fresh Shanghai-style noodles or fresh egg noodles
2   tablespoons vegetable oil
1   teaspoon minced garlic
1   leek, trimmed and cut into 1½-inch slivers
1   red bell pepper, seeded and cut into matchstick pieces
3   tablespoons soy sauce
1   tablespoon Shao Hsing wine or dry sherry
2   tablespoons sweet brown bean sauce
2   tablespoons Chinkiang vinegar or red wine vinegar
4   teaspoons sesame oil

Preparation

Combine marinade ingredients in a small bowl. Add chicken and stir to coat. Set aside for 30 minutes.

Cooking

In a large pot of boiling water, cook noodles according to package directions until tender but firm to the bite. Drain well.

Place a wok or wide frying pan over high heat until hot. Add vegetable oil, swirling to coat sides. Add garlic and cook, stirring, until fragrant, about 5 seconds. Add chicken and stir-fry for 2 minutes or until opaque. Add leek and bell pepper and cook for 1 minute. Stir in soy sauce, wine, brown bean sauce, vinegar, sesame oil, and noodles. Cook and gently toss until heated through.

Tip: Shanghai noodles are a slightly thicker version of the basic fresh Chinese egg noodles. If these are unavailable, any egg noodles may be substituted.

Eight Treasure Noodle Pancake

To a Cantonese like me, *chow mein* means just one thing — a large handful of boiled noodles, shaped into a loose disk and cooked in a skillet until well browned and crispy on both sides. The resulting noodle pancake serves as a base for a saucy stir-fried mixture. Again, just about any stir-fried dish can be served on top of a noodle pancake. (Photo, page 59)

Makes: 6 servings

6   dried black mushrooms

Sauce
⅔   cup chicken broth
3   tablespoons soy sauce
2   teaspoons sesame oil
½   teaspoon sugar

■   ■   ■

1   package (about 1 lb.) fresh egg noodles
5   tablespoons vegetable oil
2   Chinese sausages (about 2 oz. each), thinly sliced diagonally
2   stalks celery, cut into matchstick pieces
½   small red bell pepper, seeded and cut into matchstick pieces
2   cups bean sprouts
2   green onions (including tops), cut into 2-inch slivers
4   teaspoons cornstarch mixed with 2 tablespoons water

Preparation

Soak mushrooms in warm water to cover for 30 minutes; drain. Cut off and discard stems and thinly slice caps. Set aside.

Combine sauce ingredients in a small bowl and set aside.

Cooking

In a large pot of boiling water, cook noodles according to package directions until tender but firm to the bite. Drain well.

Place a wide frying pan with a nonstick finish over medium-high heat until hot. Add 1 tablespoon of the oil, swirling to coat surface. Spread half the noodles over bottom of pan. Press noodles to form a firmer pancake. Cook for 5 minutes or until bottom is golden brown. Carefully turn noodles over in one piece. Add 1 more tablespoon oil and cook for 5 minutes longer or until bottom is golden brown. Remove noodle pancake to a large heatproof serving platter and keep warm in a 200°F oven while cooking remaining noodles with 2 more tablespoons of the oil.

Place a wok or wide frying pan over high heat until hot. Add the remaining 1 tablespoon oil, swirling to coat sides. Add sausages and mushrooms and stir-fry for 1 minute. Add celery and bell pepper and cook for 1 minute. Add bean sprouts, green onions, and sauce and cook for 1 minute. Add cornstarch solution and cook, stirring, until sauce boils and thickens. To serve, spoon sausage-vegetable mixture over noodle pancakes.

Tip: If boiled noodles are not fried immediately, toss them with 2 teaspoons sesame oil to prevent noodles from sticking together.

Barbecued Duck with Vegetables and Pasta

Here is a delicious way to use leftovers of the roast duck on page 121. Actually, I seldom have leftovers of something so delicious, so I generally pick up half a duck at a Chinese take-out deli especially for this dish. Then the whole thing can be prepared and assembled in the time it takes to boil water and cook the noodles. (Photo, page 120)

Makes: 4 servings

2	baby bok choy
8	ounces dried corkscrew pasta

Sauce

1	tablespoon vegetable oil
1	teaspoon minced fresh ginger
⅓	cup chicken broth
1½	tablespoons soy sauce
1	tablespoon Shao Hsing wine or dry sherry
1	teaspoon sesame oil
1½	teaspoons cornstarch mixed with 1 tablespoon water

■   ■   ■

1	large carrot, cut into matchstick pieces
½	Cantonese roast duck (about 2 lbs.), cut into serving-size pieces

Cooking

Bring water to a boil in a medium saucepan. Plunge bok choy into boiling water for 5 minutes or until softened. Rinse under cold running water and drain well. Cut each bok choy in half lengthwise and set aside.

In a large pot of boiling water, cook noodles according to package instructions until tender but firm to the bite. Drain well and set aside.

Place a small saucepan over medium-high heat until hot. Add vegetable oil, swirling to coat surface. Add ginger and cook, stirring, until fragrant, about 5 seconds. Add broth, soy sauce, wine, and sesame oil and cook until mixture comes to a boil. Add cornstarch solution and cook, stirring, until sauce thickens.

To serve, divide pasta, carrot, bok choy, and duck among 4 plates. Serve sauce over carrot and bok choy.

Chinese Paella (page 51) ▶

Rice in a Lotus Leaf (page 47)

Eight Treasure Noodle Pancake *(page 55)*

Glass Noodles with Peanut Sauce

Peanuts are a "new" food in Chinese cooking — we've only been using them for three or four hundred years, since they were introduced from the West. Besides using them for oil, we put ground peanuts in stir-fried dishes, stuffings, and sauces like this sweet-tart-spicy topping for bean thread noodles. (Photo, opposite page)

Makes: 4 servings

Marinade
1   tablespoon soy sauce
2   teaspoons Shao Hsing wine or dry sherry

    ■   ■   ■

2   chicken breast halves, skinned, boned, and cut into matchstick pieces

Peanut Sauce
¼   cup peanut butter
3   tablespoons soy sauce
2   tablespoons rice vinegar
1   tablespoon chicken broth or water
1   tablespoon sesame oil
2   teaspoons sugar
2   teaspoons chili oil

    ■   ■   ■

8   ounces dried bean thread noodles
2   tablespoons vegetable oil
1   teaspoon minced garlic
2   teaspoons minced fresh ginger
½   medium red onion, thinly sliced
½   cucumber, peeled, seeded, and cut into matchstick pieces
1   medium carrot, shredded
½   cup unsalted roasted peanuts, coarsely chopped

Preparation

Combine marinade ingredients in a small bowl. Add chicken and stir to coat. Set aside for 30 minutes. Combine peanut sauce ingredients in another bowl and set aside.

Cooking

Bring 4 cups water to a boil in a medium saucepan. Add noodles, stirring to separate strands. Cook, stirring, for 30 seconds or until noodles are slightly soft. Pour into a colander and rinse under cold running water. Drain well, cut noodles in half, and set aside.

Place a wok or wide frying pan over high heat. Add oil, swirling to coat sides. Add garlic and ginger and cook, stirring, until fragrant, about 5 seconds. Add chicken and stir-fry for 1 minute or until opaque. Add onion and stir-fry for 1 minute. Add cucumber, carrot, and peanut sauce and cook, stirring, until slightly thickened. Remove from heat. Add noodles and toss until evenly coated. Sprinkle with peanuts.

◀ *Clockwise from top: Chinese Vegetable Pickles (page 68), Glass Noodles with Peanut Sauce, Shanghai Chow Mein (page 54)*

Chinese Noodle Soup

This is the kind of noodle soup that millions of Chinese eat for lunch every day, in the markets, in modest restaurants, or even from sidewalk carts. Feel free to improvise — use sliced ham or shredded cooked chicken in place of the barbecued pork, sliced cabbage or bok choy instead of snow peas, or whatever else strikes your fancy.

Makes: 4 servings

- 6 **dried black mushrooms**
- 1 **package (about 1 lb.) fresh egg noodles**
- 4 **cups chicken broth**
- ¼ **pound snow peas, ends snapped off and strings removed**
- 1 **small red bell pepper, seeded and cut into matchstick pieces**
- 2 **tablespoons soy sauce**
- 1 **tablespoon Shao Hsing wine or dry sherry**
- 2 **teaspoons sesame oil**
- ⅛ **teaspoon white pepper**
  Salt to taste
- ½ **pound barbecued pork, thinly sliced**
- 2 **green onions (including tops), slivered**

Preparation

Soak mushrooms in warm water to cover for 30 minutes; drain. Cut off and discard stems and thinly slice caps. Set aside.

Cooking

In a large pot of boiling water, cook noodles according to package directions until tender but firm to the bite. Drain well.

In a wok or large pot, bring broth and mushrooms to a boil over medium-high heat. Add snow peas and bell pepper and cook for 2 minutes or until snow peas are crisp-tender. Add soy sauce, wine, sesame oil, pepper, and salt and cook for 1 minute. Add noodles and cook until heated through. Transfer to a large serving bowl and top with barbecued pork and green onions.

Stone Soup with Rice Noodles

Here is an example of a less traditional noodle soup. The name comes from the legend of a beggar who claimed he could make a delicious soup from a stone. After boiling the stone in plain water for a while, he announced that he needed some vegetables, then some chicken, then some noodles … and when he was done, he threw away the stone!

Makes: 4 servings

4   **dried black mushrooms**

Marinade
1   **tablespoon Shao Hsing wine or dry sherry**
2   **teaspoons cornstarch**
½   **teaspoon salt**

■ ■ ■

2   **chicken breast halves, skinned, boned, and thinly sliced**
8½   **cups water**
8   **ounces dried rice stick noodles, broken in half**
3½   **cups chicken broth**
     Salt and pepper to taste
2   **tablespoons vegetable oil**
½   **teaspoon minced garlic**
½   **small zucchini or crookneck squash, cut into matchstick pieces**
1   **small carrot, cut into matchstick pieces**
1   **tablespoon soy sauce**
¾   **teaspoon sesame oil**
1   **teaspoon cornstarch mixed with 2 teaspoons water**
     Chili oil to taste
     Slivered green onion for garnish
     Enoki mushrooms for garnish

Preparation

Soak mushrooms in warm water to cover for 30 minutes; drain. Cut off and discard stems and thinly slice caps.

Combine marinade ingredients in a bowl. Add chicken and stir to coat. Set aside for 30 minutes.

Cooking

Bring 8 cups of the water to a boil in a large pot. Add rice stick noodles, stirring to separate strands. When water returns to a boil, add the remaining ½ cup water. Return to boil again and cook, stirring occasionally, for 1½ minutes or until noodles are tender but firm to the bite. Pour into colander and drain well. Divide noodles equally among 4 soup bowls. Set aside.

In a large pot, bring 3 cups of the chicken broth to a boil over medium-high heat. Add salt and pepper. Reduce heat to medium-low. Let simmer.

Place a wok or wide frying pan over high heat until hot. Add 1½ tablespoons of the vegetable oil, swirling to coat sides. Add chicken and stir-fry for 1½ minutes or until opaque. Remove chicken. Heat the remaining ½ tablespoon vegetable oil in wok until hot. Add mushrooms, garlic, zucchini, carrot, and the remaining ½ cup chicken broth. Cover and cook for 2 minutes or until zucchini and carrot are crisp-tender. Return chicken to wok. Stir in soy sauce and sesame oil. Add cornstarch solution and cook, stirring, until sauce boils and thickens.

Spoon chicken mixture over noodles in soup bowls; ladle broth over all. Season with chili oil and sprinkle with green onion and enoki mushrooms.

Vegetarian Cold Pasta

The Chinese eat pasta salad too! A bowl of cold noodles tossed with a flavorful dressing and finely cut vegetables makes a refreshing but substantial warm-weather lunch or an attractive side dish.

Makes: 4 servings

Dressing

2	tablespoons soy sauce
2	tablespoons red wine vinegar
2	tablespoons vegetable oil
1	tablespoon sesame oil
½	teaspoon sugar
½	teaspoon chili oil
¼	teaspoon white pepper

■ ■ ■

1	package (about 1 lb.) fresh egg noodles
1	stalk celery, cut into matchstick pieces
1	carrot, cut into matchstick pieces
2	green onions (including tops), cut into 2-inch slivers
¼	cup red-in-snow (optional)
2	tablespoons shredded Sichuan preserved vegetables

Preparation

Combine dressing ingredients in a small bowl and set aside.

Cooking

In a large pot of boiling water, cook noodles according to package instructions until tender but firm to the bite. Drain well. Transfer noodles to a large serving bowl. Top with celery, carrot, green onions, red-in-snow, and preserved vegetables. Whisk dressing ingredients to recombine and pour over pasta and vegetables. Toss well.

Tip: Red-in-snow, available in cans in Oriental grocery stores, is a pungent, aromatic preserved vegetable. The name refers to the red blossoms that appear during the snowy winter months.

VEGETABLES
AND TOFU

...

A Chinese cook can get by very nicely without meat, and if necessary, even without seafood and poultry. But Chinese cooking is almost unimaginable without an assortment of fresh vegetables.

Some Chinese vegetables are now familiar items in supermarkets; less familiar varieties are available in Asian markets in many communities. (If you are interested in growing your own Chinese vegetables, see the suggestions and seed sources on page 73.) Of course, not all the dishes in this book call for Oriental vegetables. Chinese cooks are adaptable, and we have learned to use many Western vegetables such as tomatoes, bell peppers, cabbage, lettuce, and chard.

Fresh vegetables are like fresh fish; they should not be too heavily seasoned or they will lose their simple, natural goodness. And they must not be overcooked. Some of the vegetable dishes in this chapter are cooked very quickly, just enough to heat them through. Even the slow-cooking braised dishes should cook only until the vegetables are tender, not mushy.

Also in this chapter are several recipes for tofu (bean curd), the bland, white cakes made from soybeans that are such an important source of protein in the Chinese diet. Braised, stir-fried, or deep-fried, tofu adds its distinctive texture to both meat and meatless dishes, while absorbing the flavors of the other foods.

Stir-fried Bok Choy

Sometimes the simplest approach is the best. To preserve the bright green color and fresh flavor of bok choy, I cook it very simply, with just a bit of seasoning and a final sprinkling of sesame seeds and sesame oil.

Makes: 4 servings

¾   **pound bok choy**
1   **tablespoon vegetable oil**
1   **teaspoon minced fresh ginger**
½   **teaspoon minced garlic**
¼   **teaspoon salt**
¼   **teaspoon white pepper**
3   **tablespoons chicken broth**
½   **teaspoon sesame oil**
½   **teaspoon toasted sesame seeds**

Preparation

Separate bok choy leaves; cut green leaves from white stalks. Thinly slice leaves and stalks and keep separate.

Cooking

Place a wok or wide frying pan over high heat until hot. Add vegetable oil, swirling to coat sides. Add white stalks, ginger, garlic, salt, and pepper and cook for 1 minute. Add green leaves and broth and cover and cook for 2 minutes or until crisp-tender. Stir in sesame oil and sprinkle with sesame seeds.

Tip: Bok choy stems are dense so they go in the wok first. This two-step cooking technique ensures the final dish will be evenly crisp-tender.

Braised Cabbage with Bean Thread Noodles

Braised vegetables are just as common in Chinese home cooking as stir-fried. This was one of my mother's favorite dishes when I was growing up. The bean threads absorb the juices and flavors from the cabbage, and the dried shrimp loses all its pungent, fishy aroma, leaving only a rich but subtle shrimp flavor.

Makes: 4 servings

2	ounces dried bean thread noodles
⅓	cup dried shrimp
4	dried black mushrooms
1	tablespoon vegetable oil
1	teaspoon minced garlic
¾	pound Chinese (napa) cabbage, thinly sliced
1½	cups chicken broth
2	tablespoons soy sauce
2	teaspoons Shao Hsing wine or dry sherry
1	teaspoon sesame oil Cilantro (Chinese parsley) sprigs for garnish

Preparation

In a bowl, soak noodles in warm water to cover for 10 minutes; drain. Cut noodles in half and set aside. Soak shrimp and mushrooms separately in warm water to cover for 30 minutes; drain. Cut off and discard stems of mushrooms and thinly slice caps. Set aside.

Cooking

Place a clay pot or 3-quart saucepan over medium heat until hot. Add vegetable oil, swirling to coat surface. Add shrimp and garlic and cook for 1 minute. Add cabbage and broth; cover and cook, stirring occasionally, for 2 minutes. Add mushrooms and noodles; cover and simmer over medium-low heat for 10 minutes or until most of the liquid is absorbed. Stir in soy sauce, wine, and sesame oil. Garnish with cilantro sprigs.

Chinese Vegetable Pickles

These crunchy pickles are frequently served in northern Chinese restaurants as a refreshing side dish. Most families make their own pickles as well, each a closely guarded recipe. You can make your own variation by adding more chilies or sugar or by adding other spices such as cassia, fennel, pepper, anise, or cinnamon.

Makes: 4 cups pickles

1½ tablespoons salt
2 teaspoons toasted Sichuan peppercorns
4 small dried chili peppers
½ cup boiling water
3 cups cold water
6 thin slices fresh ginger
1 tablespoon Shao Hsing wine or dry sherry, vodka, or gin
4 cups of any combination of the following, cut into bite-size pieces: carrots, daikon, cauli-flower, cucumbers, cabbage, red or green bell peppers
6 whole fresh red chili peppers

Preparation

Combine salt, peppercorns, chili peppers, and boiling water in a large bowl; stir until salt dissolves. Stir in cold water, ginger, and wine. Add vegetables and mix well. Transfer to a large glass jar or ceramic pot, cover, and refrigerate for at least 24 hours or as long as 5 days.

Variation: Chinese Sweet and Sour Vegetable Pickles

Combine 1½ tablespoons salt and vegetables in a large bowl. Cover with an inverted plate and weight down with a heavy object. Let stand for 30 minutes. Lightly rinse under cold water; drain. Squeeze vegetables to extract liquid and set aside. Combine ¾ cup rice vinegar, 2½ tablespoons sugar, and 2 teaspoons salt in a large bowl. Add vegetables and mix well. Transfer to a glass jar or ceramic pot, cover, and refrigerate overnight.

Dry-fried Green Beans with Minced Pork

"Dry-frying" is a technique of cooking stir-fried or deep-fried foods with a minimum of liquid, then boiling away that little bit of liquid until the sauce clings to the food. (Photo, page 78)

Makes: 4 servings

2 tablespoons dried shrimp

Sauce
1 tablespoon dark soy sauce
1 teaspoon soy sauce
½ teaspoon sugar
½ teaspoon sesame oil

Preparation

Soak shrimp in warm water to cover for 30 minutes; drain. Coarsely chop shrimp and set aside.

Combine sauce ingredients in a small bowl and set aside.

Vegetable oil for deep-frying
1   **pound green beans, ends removed and cut diagonally into 3-inch pieces**
1   **teaspoon minced garlic**
1   **teaspoon minced fresh ginger**
4   **whole dried red chili peppers**
½   **teaspoon crushed red pepper**
½   **pound lean ground pork**

Cooking

Set wok in a ring stand and add oil to a depth of about 2 inches. Over high heat, bring oil to 360°F. Add green beans, half at a time, and cook for 2 minutes or until beans become wrinkled. Lift out and drain on paper towels; set aside.

Remove all but 1 tablespoon oil from wok. Place wok over high heat. Add garlic, ginger, chili peppers, and crushed red pepper and cook, stirring, until fragrant, about 5 seconds. Add pork and stir-fry for 1½ minutes or until meat is browned and crumbly. Return green beans to wok. Stir in sauce and cook for 1 minute.

Tip: Be careful when adding beans to hot oil as the water from the beans will cause the oil to spatter.

Chinese Broccoli with Oyster Sauce

If you cannot get Chinese broccoli (*gai lan*), try this simple but delicious preparation with Western-style broccoli or fresh asparagus. Adjust the blanching time according to the size of the vegetables; they should be cooked through but still firm and crisp. (Photo, page 78)

Makes: 4 servings

2   **tablespoons oyster-flavored sauce**
1   **teaspoon sesame oil**
¾   **pound Chinese broccoli or regular broccoli**
8   **cups water**
2   **tablespoons vegetable oil**
1   **teaspoon salt**

Preparation

Combine oyster sauce and sesame oil in a small bowl and set aside.

Wash broccoli and peel off tough skin on stems. Remove flowerets from stems and cut into bite-size pieces. Cut stems diagonally into thin slices.

Cooking

Bring water, vegetable oil, and salt to a boil in a large pot. Plunge broccoli into boiling water and cook for 4 minutes or until crisp-tender. Drain well and place on a platter. Drizzle with oyster sauce mixture.

Stir-fried Winter Melon

The delicate flavor and texture of winter melon (somewhere between a cucumber and a very mild summer squash) make a nice background for other subtle flavors — in this case, two kinds of mushrooms. I also use both regular and dark soy sauce for this dish, because the balance of flavors is not quite right with either one alone.

Makes: 4 to 6 servings

1   **pound winter melon**
1   **tablespoon vegetable oil**
½   **teaspoon minced fresh garlic**
½   **teaspoon minced fresh ginger**
1   **small carrot, cut into ½-inch cubes**
¼   **cup Chinese vegetarian broth (page 31)**
1   **can (15 oz.) peeled straw mushrooms, drained**
¼   **pound fresh mushrooms, cut into quarters**
1   **tablespoon dark soy sauce**
1   **tablespoon soy sauce**
½   **teaspoon sesame oil**
2   **green onions (including tops), cut into ½-inch pieces**
2   **teaspoons cornstarch mixed with 4 teaspoons water**

Preparation

Remove skin and seeds from winter melon. Cut flesh into ½-inch cubes.

Cooking

Place a wok or wide frying pan over high heat until hot. Add vegetable oil, swirling to coat sides. Add garlic and ginger and cook, stirring, until fragrant, about 5 seconds. Add winter melon and carrot and cook for 30 seconds. Add broth; cover and cook for 2 minutes. Add straw mushrooms and fresh mushrooms and cook for 4 minutes or until carrot is crisp-tender. Add soy sauces, sesame oil, and green onions and cook for 30 seconds. Add cornstarch solution and cook, stirring, until sauce boils and thickens.

Swiss Chard with Black Bean Sauce

This is one stir-fry that really requires a wok. Raw chard loses a lot of volume as it cooks; in order to have enough to eat, you have to start with more raw leaves than will fit in a skillet.

Makes: 4 servings

Sauce

2	tablespoons rice vinegar
1	tablespoon soy sauce
¼	teaspoon sugar

■ ■ ■

1	large bunch Swiss chard
2	strips bacon, cut into ½-inch wide pieces
1	teaspoon minced garlic
1	tablespoon fermented black beans, rinsed and coarsely chopped
1	can (8 oz.) sliced water chestnuts, drained
1	tablespoon cornstarch mixed with 2 tablespoons water

Preparation

Combine sauce ingredients in a small bowl and set aside. Rinse chard and cut into ½-inch-wide slices.

Cooking

Place a wok over medium-high heat until hot. Add bacon and cook until crisp. Add garlic and black beans and stir-fry for 15 seconds. Add chard and water chestnuts. Cover and cook for 5 minutes or until chard is wilted. Stir in sauce. Add cornstarch solution and cook, stirring, until sauce boils and thickens.

Buddhist Delight

There is a long tradition of Buddhist vegetarian cookery in China. Vegetarian dishes full of symbolic ingredients are often served at the Chinese New Year to symbolize the desire to have a happy, harmonious, and peaceful beginning. (Photo, page 157)

Makes: 4 to 6 servings

8   **dried black mushrooms**
10 **cloud ears**
2   **dried bean curd sticks**
2   **ounces dried bean thread noodles, separated**
24 **dried tiger lily buds**
¼   **ounce black moss (optional)**

Sauce
⅔   **cup Chinese Broth (page 31)**
2   **tablespoons oyster-flavored sauce**
2   **tablespoons soy sauce**
1   **tablespoon mashed red fermented bean curd**
2   **teaspoons sesame oil**
1½ **teaspoons sugar**
½   **teaspoon salt**
¼   **teaspoon white pepper**

■ ■ ■

2   **tablespoons vegetable oil**
1   **teaspoon minced garlic**
1   **thin slice fresh ginger**
3   **green onions (including tops), cut into 1-inch pieces**
1   **small carrot, thinly sliced**
¼   **cup sliced bamboo shoots**
½   **cup sliced water chestnuts**
½   **cup canned ginkgo nuts, drained (optional)**
1   **can baby corn, drained**
½   **pound Chinese (napa) cabbage, cut into 1 x 2-inch pieces**
½   **package firm tofu, drained and cut into 1-inch cubes**

Preparation

Soak mushrooms, cloud ears, bean curd sticks, bean thread noodles, tiger lily buds, and black moss separately in warm water to cover for 30 minutes; drain. Cut off and discard mushroom stems and cut caps into quarters. Cut bean curd sticks into 1-inch pieces. Cut off hard knobby ends of lily buds and tie each bud into a knot. Rinse black moss and drain well. Set each ingredient aside separately.

Combine sauce ingredients in a small bowl and set aside.

Cooking

Place a wok or wide frying pan over high heat until hot. Add oil, swirling to coat sides. Add garlic, ginger, green onions, mushrooms, and bean curd sticks and cook for 1½ minutes. Add carrot, bamboo shoots, water chestnuts, ginkgo nuts, baby corn, and cabbage and cook for 1 minute. Add cloud ears, tiger lily buds, and black moss and cook for 30 seconds. Stir in sauce. Cover and cook for 5 minutes. Add tofu and bean thread noodles. Reduce heat to medium. Cover and cook for 12 minutes or until sauce is absorbed.

Tip: Black moss is a dried seaweed from China, consisting of hair-thin threads. It is sold in plastic envelopes in well-stocked Oriental stores. Bean curd sticks are rolled and dried sheets of the "skin" that rises to the top of soy milk in the tofu-making process. They cook to a pleasantly chewy consistency.

Growing Your Own Chinese Vegetables

Many varieties of fresh Oriental vegetables are available in local supermarkets. But if your favorites are difficult to find, or gardening is your hobby, why not try growing your own? The flavor of fresh-picked vegetables is incomparable.

Oriental vegetables can be divided into two categories: cool-weather and warm-weather. Generally, green leafy vegetables such as bok choy, Chinese mustard greens, and cilantro, as well as vegetables which mature underground such as daikon, carrots, and turnips grow well during the cooler months of early spring (or fall in mild-winter areas). Chinese broccoli and snow peas also fare well during these months.

Later in the spring, plant warm-season vegetables — gourds and squashes such as winter melon, Chinese long beans, Chinese okra — to mature in summer and fall. Consult your local nursery for appropriate planting dates for both cool and warm-weather crops.

Mung bean sprouts can be grown year round in just a few days. Sprouts purchased in grocery stores are so frequently of poor quality that the little effort involved in growing your own is worth it. To grow your own bean sprouts, wash ½ cup dried green mung beans and place in a one-quart jar with 2 cups cold water. Cover with cheesecloth and secure the cloth with string or a rubber band. The next day, drain off the water, rinse the beans, and drain again. Let stand, covered, overnight. Repeat this process for 1 or 2 more days. When the white stems reach about 2½ to 3 inches long, pick the sprouts from the jar and rinse in a large bowl of water to remove the green husks. Drain well and use within a few days.

A variety of vegetable seeds are available in Oriental stores or your local nursery. They are also available by mail from House of Tsang Inc., P.O. Box 294, Belmont, CA. 94002.

Stir-fried Pressed Bean Curd with Jicama

I love the different textures in this dish — the firm, meaty, almost chewy strips of fried bean curd next to the sweet, refreshing, crisp sticks of jicama and the tender green onions.

Makes: 4 to 6 servings

1	**tablespoon vegetable oil**
1	**package (7 oz.) pressed, flavored soy bean cake, cut into 3-inch matchstick pieces**
½	**pound jicama, peeled and cut into 3-inch matchstick pieces**
2	**green onions (including tops), cut into 2-inch pieces**
2	**tablespoons chicken broth**
½	**teaspoon salt**
½	**teaspoon sugar**
¼	**teaspoon Chinese five-spice**

Cooking

Place a wok or wide frying pan over high heat until hot. Add oil, swirling to coat sides. Add soy bean strips, jicama, and green onions and stir-fry for 1 minute. Stir in broth, salt, sugar, and five-spice. Cover and cook for 2 minutes.

Sichuan Braised Bean Curd

In this dish, originally from Sichuan province but now popular all over China, the bland flavor of tofu contrasts with a rich, thick, chili-flavored sauce studded with bits of minced pork.

Makes: 4 servings

Sauce
¼ cup chicken broth
2 tablespoons soy sauce
1 teaspoon chili paste
1 teaspoon sesame oil

■ ■ ■

2 tablespoons vegetable oil
2 teaspoons minced garlic
1 teaspoon minced fresh ginger
4 whole dried red chili peppers
1 tablespoon fermented black beans, rinsed and coarsely chopped
2 green onions (including tops), cut into 2-inch pieces
¼ pound lean ground pork
1 package (about 1 lb.) firm tofu, drained and cut into ½-inch cubes
½ cup sliced bamboo shoots
2 teaspoons cornstarch mixed with 4 teaspoons water

Preparation

Combine sauce ingredients in a small bowl and set aside.

Cooking

Place a wok or wide frying pan over high heat until hot. Add oil, swirling to coat sides. Add garlic, ginger, chili peppers, black beans, and green onions; cook, stirring, until fragrant, about 5 seconds. Add pork and stir-fry for 1½ minutes or until meat is browned and crumbly. Stir in sauce, tofu, and bamboo shoots. Cover and cook for 2 minutes. Add cornstarch solution and cook, stirring, until sauce boils and thickens.

Tip: Wash your hands well — and do not touch your face — after handling chili peppers. They contain volatile oils which may burn your skin.

Hakka Bean Curd Soup

This is a very substantial soup, more of a stew, of seafood-stuffed tofu triangles carefully arranged in a clay pot and gently braised. The Hakka are a group of Chinese whose ancestors migrated to southern China from the north, and their food is generally spicier than other southern cooking styles. (Photo, opposite page)

Makes: 4 servings

Filling

2   **ounces white fish fillets, such as sole, halibut, or lingcod**
2   **ounces medium-size raw shrimp, peeled and deveined**
2   **teaspoons vegetable oil**
1   **egg white**
1   **teaspoon cornstarch**
½   **teaspoon sesame oil**
¼   **teaspoon salt**
     Pinch of white pepper
1   **teaspoon coarsely chopped cilantro (Chinese parsley)**

■   ■   ■

4   **dried black mushrooms**
8   **dried shrimp**
1   **package (about 1 lb.) firm tofu, drained**
     Cornstarch for dry-coating
1   **tablespoon vegetable oil**
1   **teaspoon minced fresh ginger**
4   **cups loosely packed 2-inch squares Chinese (napa) cabbage**
1½   **cups chicken broth**
½   **teaspoon sesame oil**
     Cilantro (Chinese parsley) sprigs for garnish

Preparation

Place all filling ingredients except cilantro in a food processor. Process mixture until smooth; remove to a bowl. Stir in chopped cilantro. (Or finely mince fish and shrimp with a cleaver and combine with remaining filling ingredients.) Cover and refrigerate for 30 minutes.

Soak mushrooms and shrimp separately in warm water to cover for 30 minutes; drain. Cut off and discard mushroom stems. Set aside.

If tofu is in one piece, cut in half crosswise. Cut each piece in half horizontally, then cut each half diagonally to make a total of 8 triangles. On the longest side of each triangle, scoop out a ½-inch-deep depression with a spoon. Coat each depression with cornstarch. Place 1 tablespoon filling in each depression, spreading the top smoothly.

Cooking

Place a 2-quart clay pot or saucepan over medium heat. Add vegetable oil, swirling to coat surface. Add ginger and cook, stirring, until fragrant, about 5 seconds. Add cabbage and stir-fry for 30 seconds. Arrange tofu triangles, filled side up, atop cabbage. Place mushrooms and shrimp around tofu. Add broth and bring to a boil. Reduce heat, cover, and simmer for 12 minutes or until fish filling turns opaque. Just before serving, drizzle with sesame oil and garnish with cilantro sprigs.

Tip: If you have leftover filling, roll into marble-size balls and nestle between tofu triangles before cooking.

Clockwise from top: **Broccoli with Oyster Sauce** *(page 69),* **Prawns with Fragrant Tea** *(page 143),*
Dry-fried Green Beans with Minced Pork *(page 68)*

Watercress and Orange Salad *(page 84)*

79

Mu Shu Vegetables

Mu shu pork is a popular restaurant dish, but other foods can be cooked and served mu shu style as well. Here is a version made of all vegetables. For a totally meatless version, use the vegetarian broth on page 31. (Photo, opposite page)

Makes: 6 to 8 servings

4	**dried black mushrooms**
1	**cup tiger lily buds**
¼	**pound jicama, peeled**
1	**small carrot**
1	**small zucchini**
1	**stalk celery**
6-8	**Mandarin pancakes or flour tortillas**
2	**tablespoons vegetable oil**
1	**teaspoon minced garlic**
1	**teaspoon minced fresh ginger**
4	**cups loosely packed shredded cabbage**
1	**green onion (including top), thinly sliced**
¼	**cup chicken broth**
2	**tablespoons soy sauce**
1	**teaspoon sesame oil**
½	**teaspoon sugar**
½	**teaspoon cornstarch mixed with 1 teaspoon water**
¼	**cup hoisin sauce**

Preparation

Soak mushrooms and tiger lily buds separately in warm water to cover for 30 minutes; drain. Cut off and discard mushroom stems and slice caps into matchstick pieces. Cut off hard knobby ends of lily buds and tie each bud into a knot. Set mushrooms and lily buds aside.

Cut jicama, carrot, zucchini, and celery into matchstick pieces; set aside in separate bowls.

Cooking

Wrap Mandarin pancakes in a clean tea towel, place in a bamboo steamer, and heat over simmering water for 5 minutes.

Place a wok or wide frying pan over high heat until hot. Add vegetable oil, swirling to coat sides. Add garlic and ginger and cook, stirring, until fragrant, about 5 seconds. Add carrot and stir-fry for 30 seconds. Add jicama, zucchini, celery, cabbage, green onion, and broth. Cover and cook for 2 minutes or until vegetables are crisp-tender. Stir in soy sauce, sesame oil, and sugar. Add cornstarch solution and cook, stirring, until sauce boils and thickens.

To serve, spread a small amount of hoisin sauce on each pancake. Place about 3 tablespoons vegetable mixture in center of pancake. Wrap up like a burrito and eat out of hand.

Tip: Mandarin pancakes can be purchased frozen in Asian grocery stores. Otherwise, purchase flour tortillas or make your own following the recipe in my other book *Martin Yan The Chinese Chef*.

Roast Beef Salad with Chinese Dressing

Salads as we know them in the West are almost unheard of in China; vegetables are nearly always cooked. But that's no reason why we cannot enjoy Western-style salads with Chinese-inspired dressings.

Makes: 6 servings

Dressing

¼   cup rice vinegar
¼   cup vegetable oil
3   tablespoons soy sauce
2   tablespoons sesame oil
1   tablespoon Dijon-style mustard
1   tablespoon sugar
2   teaspoons minced garlic
1   teaspoon chili oil

Salad

1   small head iceberg lettuce, shredded
1   small carrot, cut into matchstick pieces
½   cucumber, peeled, seeded, and cut into matchstick pieces
½   pound roast beef, cut into thin strips
2   green onions (including tops), slivered

Preparation

Place dressing ingredients in a blender. Process mixture for 10 seconds or until smooth. Place lettuce, carrot, and cucumber in a large wide salad bowl; toss well. Arrange roast beef strips on salad. Pour dressing over roast beef and sprinkle with green onions. Toss just before serving.

Spinach Salad with Tofu Dressing

Here is another very non-Chinese salad with a creamy dressing based on tofu blended to a smooth purée. Try it on other salads, too. This is one of my favorites — it's light and healthy.

Makes: 4 to 6 servings

Dressing

4   **ounces firm tofu, drained**

¼   **cup Chinkiang vinegar or red wine vinegar**

3   **tablespoons vegetable oil**

1   **tablespoon sugar**

1   **tablespoon soy sauce**

1   **tablespoon sesame oil**

1   **teaspoon chili oil**

1   **teaspoon minced garlic**

■ ■ ■

1   **bunch spinach (about 1 lb.), washed, stems removed, and leaves torn into bite-size pieces**

5   **strips bacon, crisply cooked, drained, and crumbled**

4   **fresh shiitake mushrooms or ¼ pound fresh mushrooms, thinly sliced**

¼   **cup sliced almonds, toasted**

Preparation

Place tofu in a blender. Add remaining dressing ingredients and process until smooth and creamy.

Place spinach, bacon, mushrooms, and almonds in a salad bowl. Pour dressing over salad and toss until spinach is evenly coated. Serve immediately.

Watercress and Orange Salad

Although I grew up eating watercress, it was always cooked, in soups or other dishes. Now I love it raw, when its refreshing bitter-peppery flavor is strongest. It's especially good in a salad with sweet oranges and bland, crunchy jicama (or fresh water chestnuts, if you can get them). (Photo, page 79)

Makes: 4 servings

Dressing
3	tablespoons vegetable oil
2	tablespoons fresh orange juice
1	tablespoon sesame oil
2	teaspoons sugar
1	teaspoon grated orange peel
½	teaspoon salt
¼	teaspoon black pepper

■   ■   ■

2	bunches watercress
1	orange
¼	pound (about 1 cup) jicama, cut into matchstick pieces
1	tablespoon chopped crystallized ginger
2	teaspoons toasted sesame seeds

Preparation

Place dressing ingredients in a blender and blend until smooth. Set aside.

Break watercress into 2-inch pieces, discarding any tough stems. Peel orange. Cut crosswise into ¼-inch-thick slices and cut each slice in quarters.

Place watercress, orange, and jicama in a salad bowl. Pour dressing over salad and toss until evenly coated. Sprinkle with crystallized ginger and sesame seeds.

Tip: For a more intense orange flavor, use undiluted frozen orange juice concentrate in place of fresh orange juice.

Five-flavored Watercress Salad

In this salad, you get all the five flavors of Chinese food — the watercress provides the bitter flavor, and the dressing is sweet, sour, salty, and hot. Actually, the presentation of this dish and the particular flavor combination of garlic, ginger, soy sauce, sesame oil, and sesame seeds is more Korean than Chinese, but it goes perfectly well in a northern Chinese meal.

Makes: 4 servings

8	cups water
4	bunches watercress, tough stems removed
1	teaspoon salt
4	cups (½ lb.) bean sprouts
2	tablespoons vegetable oil
1	teaspoon minced garlic
½	teapoon minced fresh ginger
¼	teaspoon crushed red pepper
1	tablespoon rice vinegar
1	tablespoon soy sauce
2	teaspoons sesame oil
½	teaspoon sugar
1	teaspoon toasted sesame seeds

Cooking

Bring water to a boil in a large pot. Plunge watercress into boiling water and cook for 4 minutes or until tender. Remove watercress, reserving water. Rinse watercress under cold running water and drain well. Sprinkle with ½ teaspoon of the salt and squeeze well to extract most of the water. Form into a small, thick disk and place on one side of a serving platter. Bring reserved water to a boil again. Plunge bean sprouts into boiling water and cook for 2 minutes. Rinse under cold running water and drain well. Sprinkle with the remaining ½ teaspoon salt and let stand for 10 minutes. Squeeze well to extract most of the water, form into a small, thick disk, and place next to watercress. Set aside.

Place a small saucepan over high heat. Add vegetable oil, swirling to coat surface. Add garlic, ginger, and crushed red pepper and cook until fragrant, about 5 seconds. Add vinegar, soy sauce, sesame oil, and sugar and mix just to blend flavors. Transfer mixture to a blender and blend until smooth. Pour dressing over watercress and bean sprouts. Sprinkle with sesame seeds. Serve at room temperature.

Eggplant Salad

This sweet-spicy-hot salad of slippery strands of eggplant is always a favorite. Soaking large eggplants in salt water rids them of any bitterness; if you use small Oriental eggplant, you can skip this step.

Makes: 4 servings

1	**large eggplant (about 1¼ lbs.) or 4 Oriental eggplants**
5	**cups water**
2	**teaspoons salt**

Marinade

3	**tablespoons red wine vinegar or rice vinegar**
2	**tablespoons soy sauce**
2	**teaspoons sesame oil**
1½	**teaspoons sugar**
½	**teaspoon chili paste**
½	**teaspoon chili oil**

■ ■ ■

Lettuce leaves for garnish

Preparation

Peel eggplant and cut into 2 x 1 x ½-inch strips. Place in a medium bowl. Add water and salt, and toss gently to mix. Set aside for 30 minutes; drain.

Combine marinade ingredients in a small bowl and set aside.

Cooking

Place steaming rack in a wok. Pour water to just below level of rack and bring to a boil. Place eggplant strips on heatproof dish and set dish on rack. Cover and steam, adding additional water if necessary, for 20 to 30 minutes or until eggplant is tender when pierced with a fork but still holds its shape. Remove dish from steamer and let cool for 10 minutes. Drain liquid. Pour marinade over eggplant. Let stand at room temperature for 1 hour or cover and refrigerate for 4 hours or as long as overnight. To serve, line a serving platter with lettuce leaves. Using a slotted spoon, lift eggplant from marinade and place on top of lettuce.

MEATS

■ ■ ■

As I have discussed in earlier chapters, vegetables and grains are more important to the Chinese diet in terms of nutrition than any other food. But meat dishes are equally important in creating a balanced meal, with a variety of foods offering many different flavors and textures. You might say that meat (along with poultry and seafood) is the "seasoning," not the substance of the meal.

Pork is by far the most popular meat in Chinese cooking. In fact, "meat" on a Chinese menu means pork; if it is beef, a second character is added to denote "cow meat." Pigs are easily raised in a small space on kitchen and garden scraps, and many village families raise a pig or two in the back yard for their own use. The mild flavor of pork also makes it a good background for other flavors.

Beef has never played as large a part in the Chinese diet as it has in some other cultures. With a large population living on a limited amount of land, it has always been more economical to devote land to growing vegetables and grains rather than grazing cattle. Here in the West, however, where beef is more plentiful, many Chinese cook it regularly, and nearly half the recipes in this chapter are for beef.

Beef and Bean Curd Delight

Western cooks tend to think of tofu as a meat substitute, but in Chinese cooking, it is more often than not combined with meat. In this simple stir-fry, tender cubes of tofu offer a contrast in shape and texture to the meat, and they soak up the savory sauce.

Makes: 4 servings

Marinade
1   tablespoon soy sauce
2   teaspoons cornstarch
          ■   ■   ■
½   pound beef sirloin or flank steak, thinly sliced across the grain

Sauce
¼   cup chicken broth
2   tablespoons Shao Hsing wine or dry sherry
2   tablespoons oyster-flavored sauce
¼   teaspoon black pepper
          ■   ■   ■
2   tablespoons vegetable oil
1   teaspoon minced fresh ginger
1   package (about 1 lb.) soft tofu, drained and cut into ¾-inch cubes
2   green onions (including tops), thinly sliced
2   teaspoons cornstarch mixed with 1 tablespoon water

Preparation

Combine marinade ingredients in a small bowl. Add beef and stir to coat. Set aside for 30 minutes.

   Combine sauce ingredients in a small bowl and set aside.

Cooking

Place a wok or wide frying pan over high heat until hot. Add oil, swirling to coat sides. Add ginger and cook, stirring, until fragrant, about 5 seconds. Add beef and stir-fry for 2 minutes or until barely pink. Add tofu and sauce and cook, without stirring, for 1 minute or until heated through. Add green onions and cook for 30 seconds. Add cornstarch solution and cook, stirring, until sauce boils and thickens.

Sichuan Tangerine Peel Beef

Thanks to my good friend, master chef Lawrence Chu, for sharing this recipe for a fragrant and spicy-flavored dish. In restaurant cooking, the beef is cooked quickly in deep oil; this technique, known as oil-blanching, seals in the juice and keeps it especially moist and tender. At home, you can simply stir-fry the beef.

Makes: 6 to 8 servings

10   pieces dried tangerine peel

Marinade
2   tablespoons water
2   teaspoons cornstarch
2   teaspoons soy sauce
      Pinch of white pepper
      ■ ■ ■
1   pound beef sirloin or flank
      steak, thinly sliced across the
      grain

Sauce
¼   cup chicken broth
3   tablespoons soy sauce
2   tablespoons dry sherry
1   teaspoon sugar
      ■ ■ ■
2   tablespoons vegetable oil
½   teaspoon Sichuan pepper-
      corns
6   whole dried red chili
      peppers
2   cloves garlic, sliced
2   green onions (including
      tops), cut diagonally into
      ½-inch pieces

Preparation

Soak tangerine peel in warm water to cover for 30 minutes; drain and set aside.

Combine marinade ingredients in a small bowl. Add beef and stir to coat. Set aside for 30 minutes.

Combine sauce ingredients in a small bowl and set aside.

Cooking

Place a wok or wide frying pan over medium heat until hot. Add oil, swirling to coat sides. Add peppercorns and cook, stirring, until fragrant, about 5 seconds. Remove and discard peppercorns. Add chili peppers, garlic and green onions and cook, stirring, until fragrant, about 5 seconds. Increase heat to high. Add beef and stir-fry for 2 minutes or until barely pink. Add tangerine peel and sauce ingredients and cook, stirring, until sauce thickens slightly.

Steamed Pork Patty

Everybody I know claims that their mother's meat loaf is the best. Of course, I feel the same way about my mom's version. It's steamed rather than baked, not just because we had no oven when I was growing up, but because I like the moist, tender texture that steaming gives.

Makes: 4 servings

Patty Mixture
4	dried black mushrooms
¾	pound lean ground pork
½	cup chopped water chestnuts
1	green onion (including top), thinly sliced
1	egg white, lightly beaten
1	tablespoon cornstarch
1	teaspoon sesame oil
¼	teaspoon salt
⅛	teaspoon white pepper
■	■　■
1	tablespoon soy sauce

Preparation

Soak mushrooms in warm water to cover for 30 minutes; drain and reserve ¼ cup liquid. Cut off and discard stems and dice caps. Combine mushrooms, reserved mushroom soaking liquid, and remaining patty mixture ingredients in a medium bowl; mix well. Spread evenly in a 9-inch glass pie dish.

Cooking

Place steaming rack in a wok. Pour water to just below level of rack and bring to a boil. Set pie dish on rack. Cover and steam, adding additional water if necessary, for 10 minutes or until meat is no longer pink in center. Remove dish and pour off and discard pan juices. Sprinkle pork patty with soy sauce.

Tip: Steam looks harmless, but it can burn. When steaming, lift the lid away from you and let steam disperse before taking out the food.

Chinese Beef Burgers

Black mushrooms, water chestnuts, ginger, soy sauce, oyster sauce, and sesame oil give a decidedly Chinese flavor to the all-American hamburger. You could also broil or grill the burgers, but I like the slightly crunchy browned surface of this pan-fried version.

Makes: 4 servings

Beef Patties

4	dried black mushrooms
1	pound lean ground beef
½	small onion, finely chopped
½	small green bell pepper, seeded and diced
½	cup chopped water chestnuts
1	green onion, thinly sliced
2	tablespoons soy sauce
2	tablespoons oyster-flavored sauce
1	tablespoon chopped cilantro (Chinese parsley), optional
2	teaspoons sesame oil
1	teaspoon minced fresh ginger
¼	teaspoon salt
¼	teaspoon black pepper

■   ■   ■

2	teaspoons vegetable oil
	Hamburger buns, split and toasted or cooked rice or noodles

Preparation

Soak mushrooms in warm water to cover for 30 minutes; drain. Cut off and discard stems and chop caps. Combine mushrooms and remaining patty ingredients in a medium bowl and mix well. Divide mixture into 4 patties, each about 4 inches in diameter.

Cooking

Place a heavy skillet over high heat until hot. Add vegetable oil, swirling to coat surface. Add patties and cook for 3 minutes on each side for medium rare. Serve patties in buns, or serve alongside rice or noodles.

Honey-glazed Garlic Ribs

Slightly sweet and spiced with mustard, this sauce gives a beautiful sheen to quickly braised chunks of spareribs. Be sure to have the butcher cut the ribs crosswise into 2-inch sections; you can do it yourself with a cleaver, but it's more difficult and somewhat dangerous.

Makes: 4 servings

Marinade
2   tablespoons Shao Hsing wine
    or dry sherry
2   tablespoons soy sauce

    ■   ■   ■

2   pounds pork spareribs, cut
    into 2-inch lengths

Honey Glaze
2   tablespoons honey
1   tablespoon soy sauce
1½ teaspoons Dijon-style
    mustard

    ■   ■   ■

1½ tablespoons vegetable oil
4   teaspoons minced garlic
⅓   cup chicken broth
    Toasted sesame seeds for
    garnish

Preparation

Combine marinade ingredients in a large bowl. Cut spareribs between bones into individual pieces. Add to marinade and stir to coat. Cover and refrigerate for 1 hour.

Combine honey glaze ingredients in a small bowl and set aside.

Cooking

Remove spareribs from marinade and drain. Place a wok or wide frying pan over high heat until hot. Add oil, swirling to coat sides. Add garlic and cook, stirring, until fragrant, about 5 seconds. Add spareribs and stir-fry for 3 minutes. Reduce heat to medium. Add broth, cover, and simmer for 10 minutes or until spareribs are cooked through. Increase heat to medium-high. Add honey glaze mixture and cook, uncovered, stirring occasionally, for 8 minutes or until spareribs are nicely glazed. Sprinkle with toasted sesame seeds before serving.

Fragrant Beef Casserole

Lemon grass, a popular herb in Southeast Asian cooking, joins more typical Chinese ingredients in this subtly seasoned, aromatic beef stew. If you can't find fresh lemon grass, look for dried leaves in herb and tea shops — it's a common ingredient in herbal tea blends.

Makes: 4 servings

Marinade
1   tablespoon cornstarch
2   tablespoons soy sauce

■   ■   ■

1   **pound boneless beef chuck,
     cut into 1-inch cubes**
1   **small Chinese white radish
     (daikon), about 1 pound**
2   **quarter-size pieces dried
     tangerine peel**
1   **cinnamon stick**
1   **one-inch piece lemon grass,
     sliced, optional**
½   **teaspoon toasted whole
     Sichuan peppercorns**
2   **tablespoons vegetable oil**
6   **thin slices fresh ginger**
1   **cup beef broth**
1   **tablespoon soy sauce**
2   **green onions (including
     tops), cut into 2-inch pieces**
1   **tablespoon cornstarch mixed
     with 2 tablespoons water**
     Hot cooked noodles
     Parsley sprigs for garnish

Preparation

Combine marinade ingredients in a large bowl. Add beef and stir to coat. Set aside.

Peel radish and cut in half lengthwise, then cut each half diagonally into 1-inch slices.

Wrap tangerine peel, cinnamon stick, lemon grass, and peppercorns in cheesecloth and tie into a bundle.

Cooking

Place a large pot over medium-high heat until hot. Add oil, swirling to coat surface. Add ginger and cook, stirring, until fragrant, about 5 seconds. Add beef and cook, stirring occasionally, for about 2 minutes or until browned. Add broth, soy sauce, and cheesecloth bundle. Bring to a boil. Reduce heat to low, cover, and simmer for 30 minutes. Add radish, cover, and continue to simmer for about 30 minutes or until beef and radish are tender. Add green onions and cornstarch solution and cook, stirring, until sauce boils and thickens slightly. Discard bundle and serve over hot cooked noodles. Garnish with parsley sprigs.

Pork Spareribs with Black Bean Sauce

With a Chinese cleaver or other heavy knife, it's easy to separate a rack of spareribs into individual ribs for eating with your fingers. If you prefer, you can use crosscut ribs (see Honey-glazed Garlic Ribs, page 92) and eat them with chopsticks. Baby back ribs can also be substituted.

Makes: 4 servings

2   **pounds pork spareribs**

Braising Sauce
1   **cup chicken broth**
1   **tablespoon soy sauce**
1   **tablespoon Shao Hsing wine
     or dry sherry**
1   **teaspoon sugar**

     ■   ■   ■

1   **tablespoon vegetable oil**
1   **tablespoon minced garlic**
1   **teaspoon minced fresh
     ginger**
2½   **tablespoons fermented black
     beans, rinsed, drained, and
     coarsely chopped**
2   **teaspoons cornstarch mixed
     with 4 teaspoons water
     Watercress or curly endive
     for garnish**

Preparation

Cut spareribs between bones into individual pieces. Bring a large pot of water to a boil. Plunge spareribs into water, cook for 2 minutes, then drain well.

Combine braising sauce ingredients in a medium bowl and set aside.

Cooking

Place a wok or wide frying pan over high heat until hot. Add oil, swirling to coat sides. Add garlic and ginger and cook, stirring, until fragrant, about 5 seconds. Add spareribs and black beans and stir-fry for 2 minutes or until ribs are browned. Add braising sauce and bring to a boil. Reduce heat, cover, and simmer, stirring occasionally, for 30 minutes or until ribs are fork-tender. Add cornstarch solution and cook, stirring, until sauce boils and thickens. Serve over a bed of watercress or curly endive.

Red-cooked Lamb

I have included only one recipe for lamb, as this meat is not especially popular except in certain parts of northern China. Most Chinese in other regions find the taste of lamb a little too strong for their liking. "Red-cooking" usually refers to meats or poultry simmered in a rich, flavorful soy-based sauce. Here, cubes of lamb pick up the same reddish-brown color from a mixture of broth and hoisin sauce.

Makes: 4 servings

2	tablespoons vegetable oil
2	teaspoons minced garlic
1	teaspoon minced shallot
1½	pounds boneless lamb, cut into 1½-inch cubes
½	cup chicken broth
2	tablespoons hoisin sauce
1	tablepoon Shao Hsing wine or dry sherry
1	package (about 6 oz.) fried tofu, cut into 1-inch cubes
2	green onions (including tops), cut into 1-inch pieces
1	tablespoon cornstarch mixed with 2 tablespoons water

Cooking

Place a wok or wide frying pan over high heat until hot. Add oil, swirling to coat sides. Add garlic and shallot and cook, stirring, until fragrant, about 5 seconds. Add lamb and stir-fry for 3 minutes or until barely pink. Add broth, hoisin sauce, and wine. Cover and simmer over low heat for 45 minutes. Stir in tofu and green onions. Cover and simmer for 15 minutes longer or until lamb is tender. Add cornstarch solution and cook, stirring, until sauce boils and thickens.

Royal Lion's Head

These large meatballs are supposed to resemble the head of a lion, especially when served with cabbage leaves draped over them as a "mane." They are often served on special occasions to symbolize happiness. (Photo, opposite page)

Makes: 4 servings

Meatballs

2	**tablespoons dried shrimp**
1	**pound lean ground pork**
¼	**cup water chestnuts, coarsely chopped**
1	**green onion (including top), thinly sliced**
1	**egg, lightly beaten**
1½	**tablespoons cornstarch**
1½	**tablespoons soy sauce**
1	**tablespoon Shao Hsing wine or dry sherry**
½	**teaspoon sugar**

■　■　■

	Vegetable oil for deep-frying
1	**teaspoon minced fresh ginger**
1	**teaspoon minced garlic**
1½	**cups chicken broth**
1	**teaspoon sugar**
½	**teaspoon salt**
	Pinch of white pepper
8	**large Chinese (napa) cabbage leaves**
½	**teaspoon sesame oil**

Preparation

Soak shrimp in warm water to cover for 30 minutes; drain. Mince shrimp and combine with remaining meatball ingredients. Set aside for 30 minutes. Shape into 4 large meatballs, each approximately 2½ inches in diameter.

Cooking

Set wok in a ring stand and add oil to a depth of about 2 inches. Over high heat, bring oil to 350°F. Add meatballs and cook for 3 minutes or until golden brown. Lift out and drain on paper towels. Remove all but 2 tablespoons oil from wok and set wok over high heat until hot. Add ginger and garlic and cook, stirring, until fragrant, about 5 seconds. Add meatballs, broth, sugar, salt, and pepper and bring to a boil. Cover and simmer over medium-low heat for 20 minutes. Place cabbage leaves over meatballs. Cover and simmer for 15 minutes longer. Sprinkle with sesame oil before serving.

Tip: If a thicker sauce is desired, transfer cabbage and meatballs to a platter with a slotted spoon. Add 3 tablespoons cornstarch mixed with ⅓ cup water to sauce, and cook, stirring, until sauce boils and thickens.

Five-spice Broiled Pork Chops (page 108)

Qingdao Fajitas *(page 110)*

Spicy Pepper Beef

I suppose I could have called this dish "five-pepper beef," as it uses five different types of peppers. Each one gives its own special aroma or flavor, as well as making an especially colorful dish. (Photo, opposite page)

Makes: 3 or 4 servings

Marinade

2   **tablespoons soy sauce**
⅛   **teaspoon black pepper**

■   ■   ■

½   **pound beef sirloin or flank steak, thinly sliced across the grain**
3   **tablespoons vegetable oil**
½   **teaspoon minced fresh ginger**
1   **teaspoon crushed red pepper**
½   **small green bell pepper, seeded and cut into matchstick pieces**
½   **small red bell pepper, seeded and cut into matchstick pieces**
½   **teaspoon sugar**
¼   **teaspoon salt**
¼   **teaspoon black pepper**
⅛   **teaspoon ground toasted Sichuan peppercorns (optional)**
1   **teaspoon sesame oil**
     Hot cooked rice

Preparation

Combine marinade ingredients in a medium bowl. Add beef and stir to coat. Set aside for 30 minutes.

Cooking

Place a wok or wide frying pan over high heat until hot. Add 2 tablespoons of the vegetable oil, swirling to coat sides. Add ginger and crushed red pepper and cook, stirring, until fragrant, about 5 seconds. Add beef and stir-fry for 2 minutes or until barely pink. Remove beef and set aside. Add the remaining 1 tablespoon vegetable oil to wok. Add green and red bell peppers and stir-fry for 1 minute or until crisp-tender. Return beef to wok. Stir in sugar, salt, pepper, Sichuan peppercorns, and sesame oil. Serve over rice.

Cashew Pork

Quick stir-fries with diced vegetables and cubes of meat in a simple soy-and-wine sauce are typical Cantonese fare. Unsalted cashews are frequently used in Chinese cooking. If salted nuts are the only ones available, you may want to reduce the soy sauce to compensate for the salt.

Makes: 4 servings

Marinade
1   tablespoon soy sauce
2   teaspoons Shao Hsing wine or dry sherry
1   teaspoon cornstarch

■   ■   ■

½   pound boneless lean pork, cut into ½-inch cubes
2   tablespoons vegetable oil
1   teaspoon minced garlic
1   teaspoon minced fresh ginger
1   small onion, diced
1   small carrot, diced
1   stalk celery, diced
1   small zucchini, diced
½   cup chicken broth
2   tablespoons soy sauce
1   teaspoon sesame oil
½   teaspoon sugar
1   teaspoon cornstarch mixed with 2 teaspoons water
¾   cup unsalted roasted cashews or toasted blanched almonds

Preparation

Combine marinade ingredients in a small bowl. Add pork and stir to coat. Set aside for 30 minutes.

Cooking

Place a wok or wide frying pan over high heat until hot. Add vegetable oil, swirling to coat sides. Add garlic and ginger and cook, stirring, until fragrant, about 5 seconds. Add pork and stir-fry for 2 minutes or until lightly browned. Add onion, carrot, celery, zucchini, and broth. Cover and cook for 2 minutes or until carrot is crisp-tender. Add soy sauce, sesame oil, and sugar; stir well to combine. Add cornstarch solution and cook, stirring, until sauce boils and thickens. Stir in nuts just before serving.

Onion Beef

Had a busy day? Try this simple, basic stir-fry. Just pull a piece of beef from the freezer as soon as you get home and let it thaw partially (it's actually easier to slice that way). Start a pot of rice, and while the rice cooks, slice and marinate the beef. The rest of the ingredients can be cut up, assembled, and stir-fried by the time the rice is done. Serve over rice and you have a complete one-dish meal.

Makes: 4 or 5 servings

Marinade
2   tablespoons soy sauce
1   tablespoon Shao Hsing wine
     or dry sherry
2   teaspoons cornstarch
2   teaspoons sesame oil
     ■ ■ ■
¾   pound beef sirloin or flank
     steak, thinly sliced across the
     grain

Sauce
¼   cup beef broth
1½   tablespoons hoisin sauce
     Pinch of black pepper
     ■ ■ ■
2   tablespoons vegetable oil
1   teaspoon minced garlic
1   teaspoon minced fresh
     ginger
1   onion, thinly sliced
4   green onions (including
     tops), cut into 2-inch pieces
1   tablespoon cornstarch mixed
     with 2 tablespoons water

Preparation

Combine marinade ingredients in a medium bowl. Add beef and stir to coat. Set aside for 30 minutes.

Combine sauce ingredients in a small bowl and set aside.

Cooking

Place a wok or wide frying pan over high heat until hot. Add oil, swirling to coat sides. Add beef and stir-fry for 2 minutes or until barely pink. Remove beef and cover loosely to keep warm. Add garlic, ginger, onion, and green onions to wok and stir-fry for 2 minutes or until onion is crisp-tender. Stir in sauce and mix well. Add cornstarch solution and cook, stirring, until sauce boils and thickens. Transfer to serving platter. Top with beef.

Orange Ginger Beef

The sweet-tart flavor of concentrated orange juice heightens the taste of fresh ginger in this version of an old favorite. For extra flavor, add a few slices of fresh pineapple.

Makes: 4 or 5 servings

Marinade

2   **tablespoons soy sauce**

1   **tablespoon Shao Hsing wine or dry sherry**

2   **teaspoons cornstarch**

2   **teaspoons vegetable oil**

    ■   ■   ■

¾   **pound beef sirloin or flank steak, thinly sliced across the grain**

Orange Sauce

¼   **cup thawed undiluted frozen orange juice concentrate**

1   **tablespoon sugar**

1   **tablespoon soy sauce**

    ■   ■   ■

2   **tablespoons vegetable oil**

5   **thin slices fresh ginger**

1   **teaspoon cornstarch mixed with 2 teaspoons water**
    Orange slices for garnish

Preparation

Combine marinade ingredients in a medium bowl. Add beef and stir to coat. Set aside for 30 minutes.

Combine sauce ingredients in a small bowl and set aside.

Cooking

Place a wok or wide frying pan over high heat until hot. Add oil, swirling to coat sides. Add ginger slices and cook, stirring, until fragrant, about 5 seconds. Add beef and stir-fry for 2 minutes or until barely pink. Add sauce and stir-fry for 30 seconds. Add cornstarch solution and cook, stirring, until sauce boils and thickens. Garnish with orange slices.

On the set of YAN CAN COOK in the studios of KQED, San Francisco

Sweet and Sour Pork

Sweet and Sour Pork needs no introduction — it's probably on the menu of every Chinese restaurant in the Western world. But you may be surprised at how delicious a homemade version can be, especially if the sauce is not too sweet.

Makes: 4 servings

Marinade
1   **tablespoon Shao Hsing wine or dry sherry**
1   **teaspoon minced fresh ginger**
½   **teaspoon salt**

     ■   ■   ■

¾   **pound boneless lean pork, cut into ¾-inch cubes**

Sweet and Sour Sauce
⅓   **cup distilled white vinegar**
⅓   **cup packed brown sugar**
¼   **cup ketchup**
¼   **cup water**
1   **tablespoon cornstarch**
2   **teaspoons soy sauce**
1   **teaspoon chili oil**

     ■   ■   ■

1   **egg, lightly beaten**
     Cornstarch for dry-coating
     Vegetable oil for deep-frying
1   **can (11 oz.) lychee fruit**
1   **small green bell pepper, seeded and cut into 1-inch squares**
¾   **cup pineapple chunks**

Preparation

Combine marinade ingredients in a medium bowl. Add pork and stir to coat. Set aside for 30 minutes.

Combine sauce ingredients in a small saucepan and set aside.

Place egg and cornstarch in separate bowls. Dip pork in egg, then roll in cornstarch, shaking off excess.

Cooking

Set wok in a ring stand and add oil to a depth of about 2 inches. Over high heat, bring oil to 360°F. Add pork, a few pieces at a time, and cook, turning occasionally, for about 3 minutes or until golden brown. Lift out and drain on paper towels. Keep warm in a 200°F oven while cooking remaining pork.

Meanwhile, cook sauce over medium-high heat, stirring, until sauce boils and thickens. Stir in lychee, bell pepper, and pineapple. Reduce heat to low and cook for 1 minute. Arrange pork on a serving platter. Pour sauce over pork. Serve hot.

Hoisin Roast Beef

Star anise and Chinese five-spice are frequent partners for beef in Chinese cooking. Here they season a delicious roast and its hoisin-flavored gravy. Leftovers are ideal for Roast Beef Salad with Chinese Dressing on page 82.

Makes: 8 servings

Marinade
¼ cup soy sauce
¼ cup Shao Hsing wine or dry sherry
2 teaspoons minced garlic
3 whole star anise, broken into pieces
½ teaspoon black pepper
½ teaspoon Chinese five-spice
■　■　■
1 beef sirloin tip roast (about 3 lbs.)

Gravy
¼ cup water
1 tablespoon hoisin sauce

Preparation

Combine marinade ingredients in a large bowl. Add meat, turning to coat all sides. Cover and refrigerate overnight, turning occasionally.

Cooking

Preheat oven to 325°F. Remove meat from marinade and place, fat side up, on a rack in a baking pan. Reserve ¼ cup marinade for gravy and set aside. Reserve remaining marinade for basting. Roast uncovered in preheated oven for 2 hours or until internal temperature registers 140°F (for rare) on a meat thermometer. Baste occasionally during roasting. Let meat rest for 20 minutes before slicing.

To make gravy, add water to pan drippings. Stir to scrape browned particles free from pan. Transfer drippings to a small saucepan. Add reserved marinade and hoisin sauce. Place saucepan over medium-high heat and bring to a boil. Simmer for 5 minutes. Serve gravy with sliced roast beef.

Five-spice Broiled Pork Chops

Surprised to see Worcestershire sauce in a Chinese recipe? Look at the label. Its ingredients include soybeans, anchovies, tamarind, garlic, and vinegar — all common foods in Asian cuisines. (Photo, page 98)

Makes: 4 servings

1   teaspoon salt
½   teaspoon black pepper
¼   teaspoon Chinese five-spice
4   pork chops, (about 8 oz. each), cut ½-inch thick
4   teaspoons sesame oil
1   green onion (including top), slivered
     Worcestershire sauce

Preparation

Combine salt, pepper, and five-spice in a small bowl. Brush each pork chop with sesame oil, then sprinkle with five-spice mixture. Set aside for 10 minutes.

Cooking

Place pork chops on a rack in a broiling pan. Broil 3 inches below heat, turning once, for 4 minutes on each side or until meat near bone is no longer pink in center. Sprinkle with green onion and Worcestershire sauce.

Cantonese Barbecued Pork Ribs

If you don't have access to a Chinese delicatessen, here is how to make your own version of their shiny, delicious barbecued pork ribs. Use the same marinade for Cantonese-style barbecued pork known as *char siu*.

Makes: 4 servings

2   **pounds pork spareribs**

Marinade
¼   **cup soy sauce**
3   **tablespoons Shao Hsing wine or dry sherry**
2½ **tablespoons ketchup**
2½ **tablespoons hoisin sauce**
2   **teaspoons minced garlic**
2   **teaspoons minced fresh ginger**
½   **teaspoon Chinese five-spice**
¼   **teaspoon salt**

Glaze
2   **tablespoons honey**
2   **tablespoons hoisin sauce**

Preparation

Trim and discard excess fat from spareribs.

Combine marinade ingredients in a large bowl. Add spareribs, turning to coat sides. Let stand for 30 minutes or cover and refrigerate overnight.

Combine glaze ingredients in a small bowl. Set aside.

Cooking

Preheat oven to 350°F. Remove ribs from marinade; reserve marinade. Place ribs on a rack in a foil-lined baking pan. Bake in preheated oven for 30 minutes. Turn meat over, baste with reserved marinade, and continue to bake for 25 minutes or until meat is tender when pierced with a knife. Turn oven to broil. Brush glaze on both sides of ribs. Broil 3 to 4 inches below heat for 3 minutes on each side or until richly glazed.

Tip: To make Cantonese barbecued pork, use 2 pounds boneless pork shoulder. Cut meat into 2-inch-wide strips, about ½ inch thick. Marinate for 2 to 4 hours. Follow cooking directions above.

Qingdao Fajitas

Texas-style fajitas have been all the rage in the last few years, and even we Chinese cooks are getting into the act! The soy sauce in the marinade gives it a special touch. In case you're wondering about the name, it's the new spelling of the city in northeastern China formerly known as Tsingtao. It's pronounced "ching-dow." (Photo, page 99)

Makes: 12 fajitas

Marinade

¼	cup soy sauce
2	tablespoons vodka, tequila, or Shao Hsing wine
2	tablespoons lime juice
1	tablespoon hoisin sauce
1	tablespoon sesame oil
1	tablespoon minced ginger
½	teaspoon Chinese five-spice

■ ■ ■

1	pound beef sirloin or flank steak

Salsa

2	large tomatoes, coarsely chopped
½	small onion, chopped
2	Serrano chilis, seeded and minced
2	tablespoons chopped cilantro (Chinese parsley)
2	tablespoons rice vinegar
2	teaspoons chili paste
½	teaspoon salt

Sour Cream Mixture

1	cup sour cream
1	tablespoon soy sauce
1	teaspoon sesame oil
¼	teaspoon white pepper

■ ■ ■

2	cups shredded lettuce
12	flour tortillas, warmed

Preparation

Combine marinade ingredients in a sealable plastic bag. Add beef, seal bag, and turn to evenly coat. Cover and refrigerate overnight.

One hour before cooking, combine salsa ingredients and sour cream mixture ingredients in separate bowls. Refrigerate for 30 minutes.

Cooking

Lift beef from marinade, reserving marinade. Place beef on a rack in a foil-lined broiling pan. Broil 2 inches below heat, turning once, for 2 minutes on each side for medium rare. Baste occasionally with reserved marinade while broiling. Thinly slice beef. To serve, place a small portion of beef strips, lettuce, salsa, and sour cream mixture on a warm tortilla, wrap up, and eat out of hand.

To barbecue:

Remove beef from marinade, reserving marinade, and drain briefly. Place on lightly greased grill about 4 inches above a solid bed of glowing coals. Cook, turning once and basting several times with reserved marinade, for 4 minutes on each side for medium rare.

POULTRY
AND EGGS

I n this country, chicken has become so commonplace that it's easy to take it for granted. But where would Chinese cuisine be without the chicken? Where, for that matter, would most of the world's great cuisines be without this noble bird? Its lean, mild-flavored meat complements all sorts of ingredients from mild to intensely flavored.

Chinese cooking uses all parts of the chicken. Boned breast or leg meat is used for stir-frying; whole birds or parts are chopped, bone and all, into chunks for braising; wings may be cooked whole or fashioned into "drumettes" (see page 119); and bones and trimmings go into the chicken broth which is the basis of so many soups. Even the feet are cooked, to be nibbled as a dim sum treat.

If the chicken has a rival for the most popular bird in China, it would have to be the duck. Who can resist a roast duck, with its crackling-crisp skin covering moist, tender, flavorful meat? (For the classic Cantonese version of this dish, see page 121.) Or slowly braised until tender, then tossed in spicy plum sauce (page 115).

If at all possible, use fresh, locally raised poultry. Fresh chicken is available in nearly every supermarket as well as at specialty markets. Duck is also widely available frozen, but if you are near a Chinatown, chances are you can find it fresh.

Poached Chicken Legs with Two Sauces

Dipping sauces allow you to add just the amount of flavor you like to each bite of simply cooked chicken. Since they are so easy to make, why not offer more than one dipping sauce? This dish uses two, one with the deep, rich flavor of oyster sauce, the other with the punch of hot chili.

Makes: 4 to 6 servings

Dipping Sauce I
2   tablespoons soy sauce
2   tablespoons chicken broth
1   tablespoon sesame oil
½   teaspoon chili paste

Dipping Sauce II
3   tablespoons oyster-flavored sauce
2   tablespoons chicken broth
1   tablespoon sesame oil
■   ■   ■
6   thin slices fresh ginger
6   cups water
2   whole star anise
1   piece dried tangerine peel
2   green onions (including tops)
2   teaspoons salt
6   chicken drumsticks

Preparation

Combine dipping sauce ingredients in separate bowls and set aside. Crush ginger with the flat side of the cleaver.

Cooking

Combine water, ginger, star anise, tangerine peel, green onions, and salt in a large pot and bring to a boil. Add chicken and heat just to simmering. Cover and simmer for 15 minutes or until meat near bone is no longer pink when pierced. Remove chicken from liquid and drain well. Serve hot or cold with dipping sauces.

Steamed Chicken with Garlic Sauce

This dish can be served right after cooking, but it's also ideal for cooking ahead of time and serving cold. You can substitute your favorite chicken parts for the whole chicken; this amount of sauce will do for three or four legs, six drumsticks or thighs, or a dozen wings.

Makes: 4 to 6 servings

1	**whole frying chicken (about 3 lbs.)**
1	**tablespoon Shao Hsing wine or dry sherry**
1	**teaspoon salt**
1	**green onion (including top)**
1	**thin slice fresh ginger**

Sauce

2	**tablespoons vegetable oil**
2	**tablespoons minced garlic**
1	**teaspoon minced fresh ginger**
1	**green onion (including top), thinly sliced**
¼	**cup soy sauce**
1	**tablespoon chili paste or ½ teaspoon crushed red pepper**
½	**teaspoon sesame oil**

■   ■   ■

Parsley sprigs for garnish

Preparation

Lightly rub chicken inside and out with wine and salt. Place green onion and slice of ginger in body cavity.

Cooking

Place steaming rack in a wok. Pour water to just below level of rack and bring to a boil. Place chicken breast side up on a heatproof dish and set dish on rack. Cover and steam, adding additional water if necessary, for 45 minutes or until meat near thigh bone is no longer pink when pierced. Carefully lift chicken from steamer and let cool to room temperature.

To make sauce, place a small saucepan over high heat until hot. Add vegetable oil, swirling to coat sides. Add garlic, ginger, and green onion and cook, stirring, until fragrant, about 5 seconds. Remove from heat and add soy sauce, chili paste, and sesame oil.

To serve, cut chicken into serving-size pieces and arrange on a serving platter. Pour sauce over chicken. Garnish with parsley sprigs.

Chicken in a Clay Pot

This is real Chinese home cooking — my mother's home to be exact. This kind of braised chicken is as popular in China as *coq au vin* is in France. Note: Unless you are an expert with a heavy cleaver, ask the butcher to cut the chicken thighs in half for you on his band saw; or simply use boneless chicken available in the supermarkets.

Makes: 4 servings

6 **dried black mushrooms**
4 **chicken thighs, cut in half crosswise**
   Cornstarch for dry-coating

Sauce
½ **cup chicken broth**
2 **tablespoons Shao Hsing wine or dry sherry**
1 **tablespoon soy sauce**
1 **tablespoon mashed fermented bean curd (optional)**
½ **teaspoon sugar**
⅛ **teaspoon white pepper**

■ ■ ■

1 **tablespoon vegetable oil**
1 **teaspoon minced garlic**
1 **teaspoon minced fresh ginger**
2 **Chinese sausages (about 2 oz. each), thinly sliced diagonally**
3 **green onions (including tops), cut into 1½-inch pieces**
¼ **cup sliced bamboo shoots**
1 **teaspoon cornstarch mixed with 2 teaspoons water**
   Green onion slivers for garnish

Preparation

Soak mushrooms in warm water to cover for 30 minutes; drain. Cut off and discard stems and slice caps in half. Set aside.

Lightly coat chicken thighs with cornstarch. Set aside.

Combine sauce ingredients in a small bowl and stir, mashing the bean curd with the back of a spoon. Set aside.

Cooking

Place a clay pot over low heat; gradually increase heat to medium-high. Add oil, swirling to coat surface. Add garlic and ginger and cook, stirring, until fragrant, about 5 seconds. Add chicken and cook for 5 minutes on each side or until browned. Add mushrooms, sausages, green onions, bamboo shoots, and sauce. Reduce heat to medium-low. Cover and simmer, stirring occasionally, for 20 minutes or until meat near thigh bone is no longer pink when pierced. Add cornstarch solution; cook, stirring, until sauce boils and thickens. Garnish with green onion slivers.

Tip: Clay pots that are used frequently do not need to be soaked. If pot is used infrequently, soak pot first in cold water to cover for 30 minutes; drain. There is no need to dry.

Braised Duck with Plum Sauce

Duck with fruit is a favorite combination all over the world. The French use oranges, prunes, or cherries, the Spanish pears, the Hungarians quince; and in China, we use a plum sauce flavored with chili and vinegar. Browning the duck first and skimming the broth before finishing the sauce gives a nearly fat-free result.

Makes: 4 servings

1   whole duck (4 to 5 lbs.), head, wing tips, and feet removed
1½ teaspoons salt
3   green onions (including tops), cut into 2-inch pieces
2   cups chicken broth
4   thin slices fresh ginger
1   piece dried tangerine peel or 1 teaspoon grated fresh orange peel

Plum Sauce
3   tablespoons plum sauce
2   tablespoons plum wine
1   tablespoon cider vinegar
3   dried whole red chili peppers
2   teaspoons chopped crystallized ginger

■   ■   ■

Mandarin orange slices or mint leaves for garnish

Preparation
Cut duck into serving-size pieces; trim excess fat. Sprinkle duck with salt.

Cooking
Place a wok or wide frying pan with a nonstick finish over high heat until hot. Add duck and cook for 5 minutes on each side or until nicely browned. Discard pan drippings. Add green onions, broth, ginger, and tangerine peel and bring to a boil. Reduce heat, cover, and simmer for 45 minutes or until duck is tender. Remove duck. Strain broth, then skim off fat. Combine ½ cup skimmed broth and plum sauce ingredients in wok. Bring to a boil over medium-high heat. Add duck and cook for 2 minutes or until sauce reduces and coats duck. Transfer to a platter. Garnish with mandarin orange slices.

Jade Chicken

This classic banquet dish gets its name from the bright green vegetables. Thin slices of Smithfield ham suggest coral, another precious stone. Everything is seasoned with a light hand, as befits the jewel-like quality of the dish. (Photo, opposite page)

Makes: 8 servings

1   **whole frying chicken (about 3 lbs.)**

Marinade
1   **teaspoon minced fresh ginger**
1   **teaspoon thinly sliced green onion**
3   **teaspoons Shao Hsing wine or dry sherry**
½   **teaspoon salt**

■ ■ ■

½   **pound Smithfield ham, cut into ¼-inch-thick slices**

Sauce Seasoning
¼   **teaspoon salt**
1   **teaspoon white pepper**
1   **teaspoon sesame oil**

■ ■ ■

1   **tablespoon cornstarch mixed with 2 tablespoons water**
4   **cups water**
1   **teaspoon vegetable oil**
¼   **teaspoon salt**
1   **pound broccoli flowerets or baby bok choy**

Preparation

Rub ginger, green onion, half of the wine, and half of the salt in chicken body cavity. Rub the remaining wine and salt on outside of chicken. Cover and refrigerate for 2 hours.

Bring water to a boil in a small saucepan. Plunge ham into boiling water for 1 minute; drain. Cut slices into 1½-inch squares and set aside.

Combine sauce seasoning ingredients in a small bowl and set aside.

Cooking

Place steaming rack in a wok. Pour water to just below level of rack and bring to a boil. Place chicken breast side up on a heatproof dish and set dish on rack. Cover and steam, adding additional water if necessary, for 45 minutes or until meat near thigh bone is no longer pink when pierced. Turn off heat, uncover steamer, and let chicken stand until cool enough to handle. Pour off broth and reserve. Remove chicken from bone; cut meat into 1½-inch squares.

Skim fat off reserved broth. Bring ¾ cup of the broth and sauce seasoning to a boil in a small saucepan. Add cornstarch solution and cook, stirring, until sauce boils and thickens; keep warm.

Bring water, vegetable oil, and salt to a boil in a large pot. Plunge broccoli flowerets or bok choy into boiling water and cook for 3 minutes or until tender to bite; drain well.

To serve, arrange ham and chicken alternately in center of platter. Arrange broccoli or bok choy around rim. Pour warm sauce over chicken and ham.

Cutting Up and Boning Chicken, Chinese Style

1. Place chicken on its back and make an incision through the skin and meat on either side of the breastbone.

2. Turn chicken over and make another incision along backbone from neck to tail.

3. Turn chicken on its side. Sever shoulder joint, leaving wing attached to breast.

4. Anchor chicken with heel of cleaver and pull on wing to pull breast away from body. Cut through skin to separate breast (small "fillet" muscle will remain attached to body).

5. Bend leg back to break thigh joint; cut whole leg free from body. Include the small muscle on the back(the "oyster").

6. With tip of cleaver, cut along ribcage to free fillet. Grasp ligament and pull away fillet. Not shown: Place fillet on board ligament side down, hold down ligament with a fingertip, and push meat off ligament. Repeat steps 3-6 on other side of chicken.

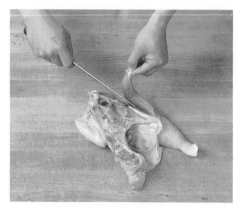

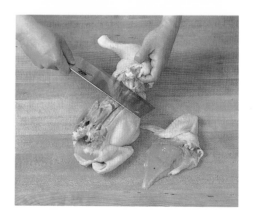

To Make Chicken Drumettes:

1. Cut off first section of wing. Cut through skin on underside of second section 1/2 inch from joint.

2. Bend wing tip back until 2 bones in second section pop out.

3. Twist smaller bone to loosen and remove. Cut off and discard wing tip.

4. With tip of knife, push and scrape meat toward other end of bone. Cut skin free from small end of first wing section and push and scrape meat to other end.

Boning Chicken Legs:

1. Cut lengthwise along inner side of leg to expose bones. With long, smooth cuts, cut meat away from bones.

2. Slide knife underneath bones to free meat from underside. Do not scrape bones, or pieces will be too small for stir-frying.

Cantonese Roast Duck

Peking Duck may be the most famous Chinese duck dish, but I like its southern cousin even better. Both have a crackling-crisp skin, from air-drying the duck prior to roasting. The Cantonese version, roasted with a liquid marinade sealed inside, is especially moist and savory. (Photo, opposite page)

Makes: 4 to 6 servings

1   **whole duck (about 4 lbs.), with head attached**

Dry Marinade
1   **teaspoon salt**
½   **teaspoon Chinese five-spice**
¼   **teaspoon ground toasted Sichuan peppercorns**

Liquid Marinade
1   **tablespoon vegetable oil**
2   **teaspoons minced garlic**
1   **tablespoon minced fresh ginger**
3   **green onions (including tops), cut into 3-inch pieces**
1   **whole star anise, broken into pieces**
2   **tablespoons hoisin sauce**
3   **tablespoons soy sauce**
1   **tablespoon Shao Hsing wine or dry sherry**
2   **teaspoons sugar**

Blanching Liquid
6   **quarts water**
⅓   **cup honey**
2   **tablespoons soy sauce**
¼   **cup Shao Hsing wine or dry sherry**
¼   **cup distilled white vinegar**

Preparation

Combine dry marinade ingredients in a small bowl and rub on outside of duck. Place duck in a pan. Cover and refrigerate for 2 hours.

Place a wok or wide frying pan over high heat until hot. Add oil, swirling to coat sides. Add garlic, ginger, and green onions and cook, stirring, until fragrant, about 5 seconds. Add remaining marinade ingredients. Reduce heat and simmer for 2 minutes. Let cool, then pour into a 1-cup measure.

Pour marinade into cavity of duck (if head and neck are missing, overlap neck skin and sew it tightly first). Sew belly opening shut with heavy thread or fasten securely with a skewer.

Combine blanching liquid ingredients in a large pot and bring to a boil. Blanch duck for 2 minutes. Lift out, drain, and pat dry. Tie a string around neck or under wings and hang in a cool place until skin is taut and dry, 4 hours to overnight (2 hours if you use an electric fan).

Cooking

Preheat oven to 400°F. Place duck breast side up on a rack in a foil-lined roasting pan. Roast in preheated oven for 30 minutes. Turn duck over. Roast for 20 minutes, brushing with pan drippings. Turn duck breast side up again and continue to cook for 10 minutes or until skin is richly browned and crispy. Continue to brush occasionally with pan drippings.

Remove duck from oven and let stand for 10 minutes. Transfer to a clean pan. Cut string and let juices from cavity drain into the pan. Transfer duck to a cutting board and cut into serving-size pieces. Skim fat from cavity juices, reheat in a small pan, and pour over duck just before serving.

◀ *Clockwise from top: Cantonese Roast Duck, Shanghai Duck Salad (page 127), Barbecued Duck with Vegetables and Pasta (page 56)*

Ballotine aux Champignons

This dish is adapted from the signature dish of my dear friend, master French chef Jacques Pepin. The procedure for boning a whole chicken with the skin intact is a bit too long to include here, but it can be found in Chef Pepin's *The Art of Cooking*. I have adapted his filling to include Chinese mushrooms, water chestnuts, and oyster sauce.

Makes: 4 servings

1 **whole frying chicken (about 3 lbs.)**

Mushroom Stuffing
10 **small dried black mushrooms**
1 **tablespoon butter or vegetable oil**
1½ **cups chopped onion**
3 **green onions (including tops), thinly sliced**
¼ **pound fresh mushrooms, chopped**
½ **cup chopped water chestnuts**
1 **tablespoon oyster-flavored sauce**
1 **teaspoon sesame oil**
¼ **teaspoon salt**
 Pinch of white pepper

Seasoning Mixture
½ **teaspoon Chinese five-spice**
¼ **teaspoon salt**
⅛ **teaspoon white pepper**

Brown Garlic Sauce
8 **cloves garlic, peeled**
1 **tablespoon soy sauce**
 Salt and pepper
2 **teaspoons cornstarch mixed with 1 tablespoon water**

Preparation

Bone chicken, leaving meat and skin intact. Remove the fillets on each side of the breast bone. Cover and set aside.

Soak black mushrooms in warm water to cover for 30 minutes; drain and reserve liquid. Cut off and discard stems and coarsely chop caps. Set aside.

Cooking

Preheat oven to 425°F.

Place a wok or wide frying pan over high heat until hot. Add butter, swirling to coat sides. Add onion and green onions and cook for 5 minutes or until onions are nicely browned. Add black mushrooms, fresh mushrooms, water chestnuts, oyster sauce, sesame oil, salt, and pepper and cook for 2 minutes or until liquid has evaporated. Let cool.

Place chicken skin side down on work surface and spread open. Sprinkle seasonings over meat. Spread stuffing on chicken and top with chicken fillets. Fold skin over meat to enclose stuffing and place seam side down. Cross legs and tie together with kitchen twine. Tie chicken to resemble a rolled roast.

Place steaming rack in wok. Pour water to just below level of rack and bring to a boil. Place chicken on a heatproof dish and set dish on rack. Cover and steam, adding additional water if necessary, for 10 minutes. Remove chicken and reserve juices.

Place chicken in roasting pan and roast in preheated oven for 30 minutes. Baste with pan juices every 10 minutes. Remove chicken from roasting pan. Remove string. Keep warm in a 150°F oven. Strain juice into a medium saucepan. Add reserved juice from the steaming process and let rest until fat comes to the surface. Skim off fat. Add reserved mushroom liquid and set aside.

Bring water to a boil in a small saucepan. Blanch garlic cloves in water for 5 minutes and drain. Add garlic and soy sauce to reserved juices. Bring to a boil and boil gently for 10 minutes. Season with salt and pepper to taste. Add cornstarch solution and cook, stirring, until sauce thickens.

To serve, place chicken on a serving platter. Spoon the garlic cloves and sauce around the chicken and serve immediately.

Chicken Cordon Rouge

Substitute shrimp and water chestnuts for Swiss cheese, add some typical Oriental seasonings, and you have a Chinese version of Chicken Cordon Bleu. But red is a more attractive color to the Chinese — it's a symbol of happiness and good fortune — so we'll call it Cordon Rouge.

Makes: 4 servings

Filling

¼ **pound medium-size raw shrimp, peeled, deveined, and coarsely chopped**
¼ **cup chopped water chestnuts**
1 **tablespoon chopped cilantro (Chinese parsley)**
2 **teaspoons soy sauce**
1 **teaspoon sesame oil**
½ **teaspoon minced ginger**
½ **teaspoon minced garlic**

■ ■ ■

¾ **cup panko (Oriental-style bread crumbs)**
¼ **cup sesame seeds**
4 **chicken breast halves, skinned and boned**
Salt and pepper
8 **tablespoons butter or margarine**
1 **ounce Smithfield ham, cut into 4 strips**

Preparation

Combine filling ingredients in a bowl; mix well and set aside. Combine panko and sesame seeds in a bowl and set aside. With flat side of a mallet, gently pound chicken breasts until each is about ¼ inch thick. Sprinkle chicken lightly with salt and pepper.

To prepare each bundle, spread 1 tablespoon softened butter across a breast about one inch from lower edge. Cover with one-fourth of shrimp filling and top with a strip of ham. Fold lower edge of breast over filling, then fold in sides and roll up to enclose filling.

Melt remaining butter in a small skillet. Dip bundles into melted butter, then roll in panko mixture until evenly coated. Place bundles seam side down, without touching, in a baking pan. Drizzle with any remaining butter. Cover and refrigerate for at least 4 hours or overnight.

Cooking

Preheat oven to 400°F. Bake chicken uncovered in preheated oven for 30 minutes or until chicken is no longer pink when pierced.

Hainan Curried Chicken

Curry spices are a fairly recent addition to Chinese cooking, but curried dishes are popular in Cantonese cooking and among the Chinese who live in Southeast Asia. This dish is named after the tropical island of Hainan southwest of Hong Kong, the only place in China where coconuts are grown commercially.

Makes: 6 servings

6   **chicken thighs**
    Salt and pepper

Curry Sauce
½   **cup coconut milk**
¼   **cup chicken broth**
2   **tablespoons Shao Hsing wine or dry sherry**
1   **tablespoon curry powder or 1½ teaspoons curry paste**
½   **teaspoon Chinese five-spice**
½   **teaspoon salt**

   ■ ■ ■

2   **tablespoons vegetable oil**
1   **teaspoon minced garlic**
5   **dried whole red chili peppers**
1   **medium onion, thinly sliced**
1   **large potato (about ¾ lb.), cut into 1-inch cubes**
2   **green onions (including tops), cut into 1-inch pieces**
2   **teaspoons cornstarch mixed with 4 teaspoons water**

Preparation

Sprinkle chicken lightly with salt and pepper. Combine curry sauce ingredients and set aside.

Cooking

Place a wok or wide frying pan over high heat until hot. Add oil, swirling to coat sides. Add chicken and cook, turning, until browned on all sides. Remove chicken from pan and set aside. Drain all but 1 tablespoon oil from pan. Add garlic, chili peppers, and onion and cook, stirring, until fragrant, about 5 seconds. Return chicken to pan. Add sauce and potato. Bring to a boil. Reduce heat, cover, and simmer for 20 minutes or until meat near bone is no longer pink when pierced. Stir in green onions. Add cornstarch solution and cook, stirring, until sauce boils and thickens.

Tip: Curry paste, a fragrant blend of spices and chilies in an oil base, is far more flavorful and complex and has a longer shelf life than curry powder. In fact, once the bottle is opened, it will keep indefinitely at room temperature. Be sure to use an Indian or Chinese brand — not the hotter Thai-style curry pastes.

Tofu with Minced Turkey

Although the Chinese raise all sorts of poultry, I never tasted turkey until I came to North America. Now I use this lean, nutritious meat frequently as an alternative to pork or chicken. Here, ground turkey takes the place of minced pork in a traditional tofu dish. Both the turkey and the tofu are low in fat and calories, making this a perfect dish for weight watchers.

Makes: 6 servings

Marinade
1   tablespoon Shao Hsing wine or dry sherry
2   teaspoons sesame oil
1   teaspoon cornstarch
¼   teaspoon salt

■   ■   ■

½   pound ground turkey
2   tablespoons vegetable oil
½   red bell pepper, seeded and diced
1   package (about 1 lb.) firm tofu, drained, and cut into ¾-inch cubes
¼   cup chicken broth
1½   tablespoons soy sauce
2   tablespoons hoisin sauce

Preparation

Combine marinade ingredients in a small bowl. Add turkey and stir to coat. Set aside for 30 minutes.

Cooking

Place a wok or wide frying pan over high heat. Add oil, swirling, to coat sides. Add turkey and stir-fry for 2 minutes or until brown and crumbly. Add bell pepper and stir-fry for 30 seconds. Add tofu, broth, soy sauce, and hoisin sauce. Stir gently and cook for 3 minutes. Transfer to a serving platter.

Sichuan Boneless Chicken

The cuisine of Sichuan province in southwestern China has become extremely popular in recent years. Here is a typical Sichuanese dish, with a hard-hitting sauce combining hot, sweet, sour, and salty flavors. The sauce also goes well with cubes of turkey, sliced pork, or small meatballs.

Makes: 4 servings

Marinade
2   tablespoons soy sauce
½   teaspoon cornstarch

■   ■   ■

3   chicken breast halves, skinned, boned, and cut into ¾-inch cubes

Sichuan Spicy Sauce
1   tablespoon soy sauce
1   tablespoon Shao Hsing wine or dry sherry
4   teaspoons rice vinegar
1   teaspoon sesame oil
1   teaspoon hot pepper sauce
¾   teaspoon sugar

■   ■   ■

3   tablespoons vegetable oil
1   teapoon minced garlic
½   teaspoon minced fresh ginger
1   green onion (including top), thinly sliced
6   whole dried red chili peppers
½   teaspoon cornstarch mixed with 1 teaspoon water

Preparation

Combine marinade ingredients in a small bowl. Add chicken and stir to coat. Set aside for 30 minutes. Combine sauce ingredients in a small bowl and set aside.

Cooking

Place a wok or wide frying pan over high heat until hot. Add 2 tablespoons of the oil, swirling to coat sides. Add chicken and stir-fry for 2 minutes or until chicken is opaque. Remove chicken and set aside. Add the remaining 1 tablespoon oil. Add garlic, ginger, green onion, and chili peppers and cook, stirring until fragrant, about 5 seconds. Stir in sauce and cornstarch solution and bring to a boil. Return chicken to wok and cook, stirring, for 1 minute or until sauce thickens.

Shanghai Duck Salad

This is a great way to make Chinese-style roast duck go further. You can use leftovers from the recipe on page 121, or buy half a duck at a Chinese deli. The spicy-sweet sauce complements the richness of the duck, and the crisp fried noodles offer a delightful crunchy texture. (Photo, page 120)

Makes: 8 servings

Dressing

3	tablespoons plum sauce
2	tablespoons vegetable oil
1	tablespoon sesame oil
2	teaspoons soy sauce
1	teaspoon Chinese mustard
¼	teaspoon chili oil

■ ■ ■

	Vegetable oil for deep-frying
1	**ounce dried rice stick noodles, broken in half**
½	**Cantonese roast duck (page 121)**
4	**cups loosely packed, shredded iceberg lettuce**
1	**cup bean sprouts**
4	**green onions (including tops), cut into 1½-inch slivers**
½	**cup shredded Chinese sweet mixed pickles or sweet gherkins**
1	**tablespoon toasted sesame seeds**
¼	**cup chopped toasted almonds**
1	**small bunch green leaf lettuce**

Preparation

Combine dressing ingredients in a bowl, whisk until smooth, and set aside.

Cooking

Set wok in a ring stand and add oil to a depth of about 2 inches. Over high heat, bring oil to 375°F. Add rice stick noodles and cook for about 5 seconds or until they puff and expand. Turn over and cook other side. Lift out and drain on paper towels and set aside.

Scrape off and discard fat under duck skin; cut skin into thin strips. Bone duck and shred meat. Combine duck meat and skin, shredded lettuce, bean sprouts, green onions, pickles, sesame seeds, and half of the almonds; toss with dressing. Add noodles and toss gently.

To serve, arrange salad on lettuce leaves. Sprinkle with remaining almonds. Serve at once while noodles are crisp.

Tip: Because brands of plum sauce vary in sweetness, start with 3 tablespoons, then taste to see if more is needed.

Golden Chicken Drumettes

Drumettes are a fancy way of dressing up chicken wings (see page 119). Baked with a crunchy, nutty coating, they make excellent appetizers or party food. Other cuts of chicken are also delicious cooked in the same ingredients.

Makes: 4 servings

Marinade

3	tablespoons soy sauce
1	green onion (including top), minced
3	teaspoons minced garlic
1	teaspoon minced fresh ginger
½	teaspoon black pepper

■ ■ ■

14	chicken drumettes
1	cup corn flakes, crushed
½	cup finely chopped walnuts
¼	cup wheat germ
	Flour for dry-coating
2	egg whites, lightly beaten

Preparation

Combine marinade ingredients in a large bowl. Add drumettes and stir to coat. Set aside for 30 minutes.

In a shallow bowl, combine crushed corn flakes, walnuts, and wheat germ. Dip drumettes in flour, then in egg whites. Roll in corn flake mixture, shaking off excess.

Cooking

Preheat oven to 350°F. Place drumettes, without touching, in a 9 x 13-inch baking dish. Bake in preheated oven for 25 minutes or until meat near bone is no longer pink when pierced.

Chicken with Fragrant Fruit Sauce

Fresh lychees from the Orient are now available in some North American markets from July to early September. Otherwise, use canned lychees in this delicious sauce for walnut-coated balls of minced chicken. It's a contemporary rendition of sweet and sour dishes as served in the most modern Cantonese restaurants in Hong Kong. (Photo, page 17)

Makes: 4 to 6 servings

6	chicken thighs (about 1 lb.), skinned and boned
1	tablespoon soy sauce
1	tablespoon Shao Hsing wine or dry sherry
1	egg white
1½	teaspoons cornstarch
1	teaspoon minced fresh ginger
¼	teaspoon salt
1¼	cups finely chopped walnuts or almonds
	Vegetable oil for deep-frying

Fragrant Fruit Sauce

1	can (11 oz.) lychee fruit
⅓	cup ketchup
⅓	cup lemon juice
1	tablespoon sugar
2	cups melon balls (cantaloupe, honeydew, or a mixture)
2	teaspoons cornstarch mixed with 4 teaspoons water

■ ■ ■

Fresh mint leaves for garnish

Preparation

Place chicken, soy sauce, wine, egg white, cornstarch, ginger, and salt in a food processor. Process mixture until smooth; remove to a bowl. Shape into approximately 16 balls, each about 1½ inches in diameter. Roll balls in walnuts to coat evenly.

Cooking

Set wok in a ring stand and add oil to a depth of about 2 inches. Over high heat, bring oil to 360°F. Add chicken balls, a few at a time, and cook for 5 minutes or until lightly browned. Lift out and drain on paper towels. Repeat until all chicken balls are cooked. Keep warm in a 200°F oven.

Drain lychees and pour ¾ cup of their syrup into a medium saucepan. Add ketchup, lemon juice, and sugar. Bring sauce to a boil. Add lychee fruit, melon balls, and cornstarch solution. Cook, stirring, until sauce boils and thickens. Arrange chicken balls on a platter. Pour sauce over chicken. Garnish with mint leaves.

Chinese Ham Omelet

In a French omelet, the eggs are cooked first by themselves, then the filling is folded inside. The Chinese way is to combine the filling ingredients with the beaten eggs and cook all at once.

Makes: 4 servings

6	**eggs, lightly beaten**
½	**cup diced cooked ham**
½	**green bell pepper, seeded and diced**
1	**green onion (including top), thinly sliced**
3	**tablespoons diced water chestnuts**
1	**tablespoon chopped cilantro (Chinese parsley)**
¾	**teaspoon salt**
½	**teaspoon chili paste**
¼	**teaspoon white pepper**
4	**teaspoons vegetable oil**

Preparation

Combine all ingredients except oil in a medium bowl.

Cooking

Place an 8-inch frying pan with a nonstick finish over medium-high heat until hot. Add 2 teaspoons of the oil, swirling to coat surface. Pour in half the egg mixture. As edges begin to set, lift with a spatula and shake or tilt pan to let uncooked egg flow underneath. When egg no longer flows freely, run a spatula around edge, fold omelet in half, and slide onto a warm serving plate. Cover loosely to keep warm. Heat the remaining 2 teaspoons oil in pan. Repeat cooking with the remaining egg mixture.

Frittata with Barbecued Pork

A frittata is an Italian baked or broiled omelet. Larger and thicker than a French omelet, it is meant to be cut into wedges to serve several people.

Makes: 4 servings

7	**eggs**
2	**tablespoons chicken broth**
1½	**teaspoons sesame oil**
¾	**teaspoon salt**
¼	**teaspoon white pepper**
2	**tablespoons vegetable oil**
1	**teaspoon minced fresh ginger**
½	**small red bell pepper, seeded and diced**
2	**green onions (including tops), thinly sliced**
½	**cup chopped bamboo shoots**
½	**cup diced barbecued pork**

Preparation

Combine eggs, broth, sesame oil, salt, and pepper in a medium bowl. Mix well and set aside.

Cooking

Place a 10-inch frying pan with a heatproof handle over medium-high heat. Add vegetable oil, swirling to coat surface. Add ginger and cook, stirring until fragrant, about 5 seconds. Add bell pepper and green onions and stir-fry for 1 minute or until crisp-tender. Add bamboo shoots and pork and cook, stirring, for 1 minute. Reduce heat to medium. Pour egg mixture into pan and cook without stirring. As egg mixture begins to set, lift edges with a spatula and tilt pan to allow uncooked egg to flow underneath. Continue cooking for 3 minutes or until eggs are softly set and top still looks moist and creamy. Remove from heat. Turn oven to broil. Place pan about 6 inches below heat and broil for 3 minutes or until egg surface is lightly set. Cut into wedges to serve.

Tip: A well-seasoned cast iron pan or nonstick frying pan is best for cooking this frittata.

Water Lily Eggs

Steaming eggs is not a well known technique in the West, but it gives a very delicate, silky-smooth texture. For a more substantial dish, add diced ham, shredded cooked chicken, or dried shrimp that have been soaked in water to soften them. Be sure to steam eggs gently, or they will come out dry and tough.

Makes: 4 servings

4   eggs
1   green onion (including top), thinly sliced
1   teaspoon Shao Hsing wine or dry sherry
1   teaspoon vegetable oil
½   teaspoon salt
⅛   teaspoon sugar
⅛   teaspoon white pepper
1½   cups chicken broth
1   teaspoon soy sauce or oyster-flavored sauce

Preparation

Combine eggs, green onion, wine, oil, salt, sugar, and pepper in a bowl; mix well. Slowly add broth, stirring constantly, and set aside.

Cooking

Place steaming rack in a wok. Pour water to just below level of rack and bring to a boil. Reduce heat so water simmers gently. Pour egg mixture into a 9-inch glass pie dish or other shallow heatproof dish and set dish on rack. Cover and steam over simmering water for 25 minutes or until a knife inserted in center of custard comes out clean. Sprinkle with soy sauce or oyster sauce.

Tip: Do not allow water in wok to boil vigorously or eggs will not be creamy.

SEAFOOD

...

Since prehistoric times, most of the settlements in China have been near water. Fish and shellfish from the sea, rivers, lakes, and ponds still provide many of the best-loved and most important foods on the Chinese table. Even in many inland areas, dried fish and shellfish imported from coastal areas provide an important source of protein.

If you really want to cook the way the Chinese do, go out of your way to find the best and freshest fish available. (In some Chinese markets and restaurants, the fish are kept alive in tanks, so you really know they are fresh!) The recipes give some suggestions for types of fish to buy, but use whatever is fresh and in season, and you cannot go wrong. And remember the basic rule — if it smells "fishy" it's not fresh. Good fresh fish should smell like an ocean breeze.

Shrimp (also known as prawns) are one of my favorite kinds of seafood, and I use them in many recipes throughout this book. If fresh shrimp are available in your area, by all means use them, but frozen shrimp are generally of very high quality. Unless otherwise noted in the recipe, buy uncooked, unpeeled shrimp.

Red Envelope Fish

Red is a lucky color to the Chinese. During the New Year's celebration, we exchange gifts in red envelopes to ensure good fortune. In this dish, a spicy sweet and sour red sauce is the "red envelope" bearing a gift of succulent deep-fried fish fillets. (Photo, page 157)

Makes: 4 servings

Sauce

½   **cup slivered Chinese sweet mixed pickles or sweet gherkins, drained**

¼   **cup sugar**

¼   **cup red wine vinegar**

2   **tablespoons ketchup**

1½ **tablespoons soy sauce**

¾   **teaspoon hot pepper sauce**

1   **tablespoon cornstarch mixed with 2 tablespoons water**

■   ■   ■

1½ **pounds mild-flavored firm white fish fillets such as red snapper, halibut, or sea bass, each about ¾-inch thick**

    Salt and pepper

1   **egg, lightly beaten**

    Flour for dry-coating

    Vegetable oil for deep-frying

    Slivered green onion for garnish

Preparation

Combine sauce ingredients in a small saucepan. Place over medium-high heat and cook, stirring, until sauce boils and thickens slightly. Keep warm while preparing fish.

Cutting only ½ inch deep into fish, score fillets lengthwise at 1-inch intervals. Then score fish crosswise at 1-inch intervals. Lightly sprinkle fish with salt and pepper. Place egg and flour in separate shallow bowls. Dip fish in egg, drain briefly, then dredge with flour, shaking off excess. Set aside.

Cooking

Set wok in a ring stand and add oil to a depth of about 2 inches. Over high heat, bring oil to 375°F. Slowly dip fish fillets into hot oil and cook, turning occasionally, for 3 minutes or until golden brown. Lift out and drain on paper towels. Transfer to a platter. Pour warm sauce over fish. Garnish with green onion.

Chinese Blackened Fish

If Chef Paul Prudhomme had been born Chinese rather than Cajun, perhaps this is how his famous Blackened Fish would taste. Don't try this dish indoors unless you have a good exhaust fan; otherwise, cook it outdoors on a portable stove. (Photo, page 138)

Makes: 4 servings

Marinade
2   tablespoons soy sauce
2   tablespoons dark soy sauce
1   tablespoon Shao Hsing wine
    or dry sherry
1   tablespoon lemon juice
½   teaspoon Chinese five-spice

    ■   ■   ■

1   pound firm fish fillets, such
    as rock cod, red snapper,
    halibut, or salmon, each
    about ¾-inch thick

Blackened Seasoning
2   teaspoons ground black
    pepper
1½ teaspoons chili powder
1   teaspoon ground toasted
    Sichuan peppercorns
¾   teaspoon Chinese five-spice
¾   teaspoon salt

    ■   ■   ■

2   teaspoons sesame oil
1   tablespoon vegetable oil

Preparation

Combine marinade ingredients in a glass baking dish. Add fish, turning to coat both sides. Cover and refrigerate, turning occasionally, for 4 hours.

Combine blackened seasoning ingredients in a small bowl.

Lift fillets from marinade, drain briefly, and pat dry. Brush sesame oil over each fillet and sprinkle blackened seasoning evenly on both sides.

Cooking

Turn on exhaust fan. Place a wide cast iron skillet over high heat for 5 minutes or until a white haze appears and skillet begins to smoke. Add vegetable oil, swirling to coat surface. Carefully place fish fillets in skillet in a single layer and cook for 2 minutes. (Oil may spatter.) Turn fillets over and cook for 2 more minutes or until center of fish is opaque and flesh has lost its wet look. Add a few more drops vegetable oil to skillet if needed.

Braised Whole Fish with Pork Sauce

Fish and pork are so prevalent throughout Chinese cooking, it's no surprise that they are often combined in the same dish. A little ground pork gives flavor and richness to many a dish of lean, delicately flavored fish. You can also prepare this with fish fillets. (Photo, opposite page)

Makes: 2 or 3 servings

2   **dried black mushrooms**

Pork Marinade
1   **tablespoon soy sauce**
1   **tablespoon Shao Hsing wine or dry sherry**
1   **teaspoon cornstarch**
         ■   ■   ■
¼   **pound lean ground pork**
1   **whole fish (about 1½ lbs.), such as trout, sea bass, or rock cod, cleaned and scaled**
      Salt and pepper
      Cornstarch for dry-coating
2   **tablespoons vegetable oil**
1   **tablespoon shredded fresh ginger**
½   **cup chicken broth**
1   **tablespoon soy sauce or brown bean sauce**
1   **teaspoon cornstarch mixed with 2 teaspoons water**
      Slivered green onion for garnish

Preparation

Soak mushrooms in warm water to cover for 30 minutes; drain. Cut off and discard stems and thinly slice caps. Set aside. Combine marinade ingredients in a small bowl; add pork and stir to coat. Set aside for 30 minutes.

Cooking

Sprinkle fish lightly with salt and pepper; lightly coat with cornstarch. Place a wide frying pan with a nonstick finish over medium-high heat. Add 1 tablespoon of the oil, swirling to coat surface. Add fish; cover and cook for 3 minutes on each side or until golden brown. Remove fish and set aside. Add the remaining 1 tablespoon oil to pan. Add ginger and cook, stirring, until fragrant, about 5 seconds. Add pork and stir-fry for 2 minutes or until meat is browned and crumbly. Add broth, mushrooms, and soy sauce and cook for 30 seconds. Add cornstarch solution and cook, stirring, until sauce boils and thickens. Return fish to pan and spoon sauce over fish. Cover and simmer for 3 minutes or until center of fish is opaque. Transfer fish to a platter; spoon sauce over fish. Garnish with green onion.

Chinese Blackened Fish *(page 135)*

Chinese Cioppino (page 145)

Lovers' Prawns

Why settle for a dish with just one sauce when you can have two? In this case, half the shrimp are served with a simple salt and pepper seasoning, while the other half get a spicy red sauce. It's an entrée for two people to share, sampling first one side, then the other. (Photo, opposite page)

Makes: 4 servings

Marinade

2   teaspoons cornstarch
1   teaspoon sesame oil
¼   teaspoon salt
     Pinch of white pepper

■   ■   ■

¾   pound medium-size raw shrimp, peeled and deveined
1   cup broccoli flowerets
2   tablespoons vegetable oil
1   teaspoon minced garlic
1   tablespoon Shao Hsing wine or dry sherry
     Salt to taste
     Pinch of white pepper
3   tablespoons ketchup
2   teaspoons rice vinegar or lemon juice
½   teaspoon sugar
½   teaspoon chili paste or hot pepper sauce

Preparation

Combine marinade ingredients in a medium bowl. Add shrimp and stir to coat. Set aside for 30 minutes.

Bring 2 inches of water to a boil in a medium saucepan. Add broccoli and cook for 1½ minutes or until crisp-tender. Drain, rinse under cold running water, and drain again. Arrange broccoli in center of a serving platter.

Cooking

Place a wok or wide frying pan over high heat until hot. Add oil, swirling to coat sides. Add garlic and cook, stirring, until fragrant, about 5 seconds. Add shrimp and stir-fry for 2 minutes or until shrimp feel firm and turn pink. Remove half of shrimp and set aside. To remaining shrimp add wine, salt, and pepper. Stir once, then place shrimp on one side of serving platter. Return reserved shrimp to pan; stir in ketchup, vinegar, sugar, and chili paste. Heat through, then place on opposite side of platter.

◀ *Upper left: Ginseng Chicken Soup (page 34). On plates: Lovers' Prawns, Sizzling Gingered Oysters (page 150)*

Fish Fillets with Ginger-wine Sauce

Steaming is one of the simplest methods of cooking fish, and the best one for preserving the delicate flavor and texture of really fresh fish. This dish works equally well with a small whole fish or slices from a larger one — just make sure it will fit inside your steamer before you boil the water.

Makes: 4 servings

Ginger-wine Sauce
¼ cup Shao Hsing wine or dry sherry
3 tablespoons chicken broth
1 tablespoon soy sauce
2 teaspoons vegetable oil
1 teaspoon sugar
   Pinch of white pepper

■ ■ ■

1 pound firm white fish fillets or steaks, such as red snapper, cod, or halibut, each about ¾-inch thick
   Salt and white pepper
1 tablespoon slivered fresh ginger
1 teaspoon cornstarch mixed with 2 teaspoons water
   Slivered green onion for garnish

Preparation

Combine sauce ingredients in a saucepan and set aside.

Cut fish into serving-size pieces. Sprinkle fish lightly with salt and pepper and place in a heatproof dish. Top with ginger and set aside.

Cooking

Place steaming rack in a wok. Pour water to just below level of rack and bring to a boil. Place dish on rack. Cover and steam, adding additional water if necessary, for 6 minutes or until center of fish is opaque. Remove dish and pour off liquid.

Place sauce over high heat and bring to a boil. Add cornstarch solution and cook, stirring, until sauce boils and thickens. Arrange fish on a platter. Pour sauce over fish and garnish with green onion.

Tip: As a rule of thumb for steaming fish, allow 10 minutes of cooking time per inch of thickness. For example, a ½-inch-thick fillet will cook in 5 minutes; a whole fish 1½ inches thick will cook in 15 minutes.

Prawns with Fragrant Tea

We usually think of tea just as a beverage, but tea leaves can also be used as a flavoring ingredient. In this dish, simply steamed prawns are served with a sauce subtly flavored with ground semi-fermented (oolong) tea. (Photo, page 78)

Makes: 4 servings

Marinade

1   egg white, lightly beaten
2   teaspoons cornstarch
2   teaspoons Shao Hsing wine
    or dry sherry
¼   teaspoon salt
    Pinch of white pepper

■ ■ ■

¾   pound medium-size raw
    shrimp, peeled (leaving tail
    intact) and deveined
¼   cup chicken broth
1   tablespoon Shao Hsing wine
    or dry sherry
1½ teaspoons quality ground
    Chinese oolong tea
¼   teaspoon sugar
    Pinch of white pepper
    Mint leaves for garnish

Preparation

Combine marinade ingredients in a bowl. Add shrimp and stir to coat. Set aside for 30 minutes.

Cooking

Place steaming rack in a wok. Pour water to just below level of rack and bring to a boil. Place shrimp in a heatproof dish and set dish on rack. Cover and steam for 7 minutes or until shrimp feel firm and turn pink. While shrimp are steaming, combine broth, wine, tea, sugar, and pepper in a small saucepan and bring to a boil; reduce heat and keep warm.

To serve, pour sauce in center of a round platter. Arrange shrimp on sauce. Garnish with mint leaves.

Tip: Try using orange spice tea in place of fermented green tea.

Fresh Crab with Ginger and Scallions

In California where I live, we are lucky to have live Dungeness crabs in our markets most of the year. Many Chinese restaurants have saltwater tanks where the crabs are kept alive until just before cooking, for the freshest possible dish. In other parts of the country, use several of the smaller blue crabs, or whatever live crabs are available. Lobster is also delicious this way.

Makes: 4 servings

1	live Dungeness crab (1½ to 2 pounds)
2	tablespoons vegetable oil
6	quarter-size slices fresh ginger
2	teaspoons minced garlic
4	green onions (including tops), cut diagonally into 2-inch pieces
¼	teaspoon salt
½	cup chicken broth
1	teaspoon sugar
1	tablespoon soy sauce
1	tablespoon Shao Hsing wine or dry sherry
4	teaspoons cornstarch mixed with 2 tablespoons water

Preparation

To kill the crab, hold crab from the rear and place crab on its back. Place the tip of a heavy cleaver on the middle of the crab's body. Hit the top blade of the cleaver with a hammer so that the blade will pierce the crab, killing it instantly.

For an alternate method, bring a large pot of water to a boil. Immerse the live crab and cook for 2 to 3 minutes. Remove crab and cool quickly under cold running water.

Pull off large top shell in one piece. Remove and discard gills and spongy parts under shell. Rinse shell and body of crab. With a cleaver, cut body into 6 parts. Twist off large pincers and break off legs. Set aside.

Cooking

Place a wok or wide frying pan over high heat until hot. Add oil, swirling to coat sides. Add ginger, garlic, green onions, and salt and cook, stirring, for 1 minute or until fragrant. Add crab body and legs. Stir-fry for 30 seconds. Add top shell, broth, and sugar. Cover and cook for 6 minutes. Add soy sauce, wine, and cornstarch solution and cook, stirring, until sauce boils and thickens.

Arrange crab legs and body pieces on a platter. Set top shell over crab to serve as a garnish.

Tip: This is messy to eat but well worth the effort. Pass a basket of damp hot towels at the table for wiping hands.

Chinese Cioppino

Cioppino, a tomato-based stew of crab and other shellfish, is one of the most famous and popular dishes along San Francisco's Fisherman's Wharf. Never one to be bound by tradition, I have taken this classic dish and given it a few Oriental touches. (Photo, page 139)

Makes: 4 servings

1	cooked Dungeness or other hard-shelled crab in shell (about 2 lbs.), cleaned and cracked
2	tablespoons vegetable oil
1	medium-size onion, finely chopped
1	small green bell pepper, seeded and diced
2	teaspoons minced garlic
1	teaspoon minced fresh ginger
2	large tomatoes, peeled, seeded, and chopped
2½	cups chicken broth
1	cup water
¼	cup Shao Hsing wine or dry sherry
8	hard-shell clams, scrubbed
½	pound medium-size raw shrimp, peeled and deveined
⅓	cup white miso or ¼ cup brown bean sauce
½	teaspoon chili paste
2	tablespoons chopped cilantro (Chinese parsley)

Preparation

Cut crab in serving-size pieces and set aside.

Cooking

Heat oil in a 5-quart pot over medium heat. Add onion, bell pepper, garlic, and ginger and cook, stirring frequently, until onion is soft. Add tomatoes and cook for 2 minutes. Add broth, water, and wine and bring to a boil. Reduce heat to low; cover and simmer for 20 minutes. Add clams. Cover and simmer for 6 minutes or until clam shells open. Add shrimp and crab. Cover and simmer for 4 minutes or until shrimp feel firm and turn pink and crab is heated through. Stir in miso and chili paste. Ladle into a serving bowl, discarding any unopened clams. Sprinkle with cilantro.

Tip: For a more intense crab flavor, take a tip from Chinese chefs and start with a live crab (see opposite page for directions on cleaning and cracking a live crab). Add crab to pot at the same time you add the clams.

Poached Fish Fillets with Soy Dressing

This is Chinese fish cooking pared down to its absolute essentials — good fresh fish, ginger, green onion, and wine, with a touch of aromatic sesame oil.

Makes: 4 servings

Sauce

2   **tablespoons soy sauce**

1   **tablespoon Shao Hsing wine or dry sherry**

2   **teaspoons sesame oil**

■   ■   ■

4   **thin slices fresh ginger**

2   **green onions (including tops), cut in half**

1   **pound firm white fish fillets, such as cod, halibut, or sea bass, ½ to ¾ inch thick**

Preparation

Place sauce ingredients in a small saucepan. Whisk until blended and set aside.

Cooking

Pour water into a wide frying pan to a depth of 2 inches. Add ginger and green onions and bring to a boil. Reduce heat so water barely simmers. Add fish, cover, and simmer for 5 minutes or until center of fish is opaque. Lift out fish with a slotted spatula, drain briefly, and place on a serving platter.

Bring sauce ingredients to a boil. Drizzle sauce over fish.

Sweet and Sour Fish

Some cooks are surprised to see ketchup used in Chinese cooking. They might be less surprised if they knew that the name (and the condiment) came from Asia in the first place. *Ketjap* (or *kecap*, both pronounced the same) is a Malay word meaning "seasoned sauce."

Makes: 4 servings

1¼ **pounds firm white fish fillets, such as cod, sea bass, or halibut, cut into 1½ x 2-inch strips**
½ **teaspoon salt**
¼ **teaspoon white pepper**

Sweet and Sour Sauce
½ **cup water**
½ **cup distilled white vinegar**
⅓ **cup packed brown sugar**
¼ **cup Chinese pickled cucumber (optional)**
3 **tablespoons ketchup**
¼ **teaspoon salt**
¼ **teaspoon hot pepper sauce**
 Pinch of white pepper

■   ■   ■

 Flour for dry-coating
1 **egg, lightly beaten**
 Cornstarch for dry-coating
 Vegetable oil for deep-frying
½ **small carrot, cut into matchstick pieces**
1 **green onion (including top), cut into 2-inch slivers**
2 **teaspoons cornstarch mixed with 1 tablespoon water**

Preparation

Sprinkle fish with salt and pepper and set aside.

Combine sweet and sour sauce ingredients in a medium bowl and set aside.

Place flour, egg, and cornstarch in separate bowls. Coat each piece of fish with flour, shaking off the excess. Dip fish in egg, then dredge with cornstarch. Set aside for 10 minutes.

Cooking

Set wok in a ring stand and add oil to a depth of about 2 inches. Over high heat, bring oil to 360°F. Add fish, a few pieces at a time, and cook for 4 minutes or until golden brown. Lift out and drain on paper towels. Keep warm in a 200°F oven while cooking remaining fish.

Bring sauce to a boil over medium-high heat. Add carrot and green onion and cook for 30 seconds. Add cornstarch solution and cook, stirring, until sauce boils and thickens.

Pour sauce on a platter. Arrange fish over sauce and serve immediately.

Double Prawns in Spicy Tomato Sauce

In some parts of the country, large shrimp are called prawns, and smaller ones are called shrimp. In other areas, all sizes are called shrimp. Are you still with me? Okay, so Double Prawns means large shrimp stuffed with a paste of smaller shrimp and deep-fried. If you prefer, you can call them Double Shrimp.

Makes: 5 servings

Shrimp Filling
2	dried black mushrooms
½	pound medium-size raw shrimp, peeled, deveined, and minced
1½	teaspoons cornstarch
1	egg white
1	teaspoon Shao Hsing wine or dry sherry
½	teaspoon minced fresh ginger
⅛	teaspoon salt
	Pinch of white pepper

■ ■ ■

10	jumbo raw prawns (10 to 12 per pound)
	Salt and white pepper
	Cornstarch for dry-coating

Spicy Tomato Sauce
⅔	cup chicken broth
½	cup ketchup
2	tablespoons lemon juice
1½	tablespoons sugar
1	tablespoon soy sauce
2	teaspoons Chinese mustard

■ ■ ■

	Vegetable oil for deep-frying
1	teaspoon minced garlic
	Tomato wedges for garnish

Preparation

Soak mushrooms in warm water to cover for 30 minutes; drain. Cut off and discard stems and finely chop caps. Combine mushrooms and remaining filling ingredients in a medium bowl. Set aside.

Remove prawn shells, leaving tail sections intact. Butterfly each prawn by making a slit on the outer side of prawn and cutting almost to, but not through, inner side. Remove sand vein. Flatten each prawn with side of cleaver blade. Lightly sprinkle prawns with salt and white pepper. Stuff each prawn with 1½ tablespoons of filling. Evenly coat prawns with cornstarch. Let stand for 5 minutes.

Combine spicy tomato sauce ingredients in a small bowl and set aside.

Cooking

Set wok in a ring stand and add oil to a depth of about 2 inches. Over high heat, bring oil to 360°F. Add prawns, half at a time, and cook for 3 minutes or until prawns feel firm and turn pink. Lift out and drain on paper towels. Keep warm in a 200°F oven while cooking remaining prawns.

Remove all but 1 tablespoon oil from wok. Reheat oil over high heat until hot. Add garlic and cook, stirring, until fragrant, about 5 seconds. Stir in spicy tomato sauce and cook until hot. Pour sauce on a platter. Arrange prawns on top of sauce.

Tip: Some Chinese cooks prefer to leave the shells on the prawns because the shells intensify the fresh-from-the-sea flavor. If you wish to do so, peel off prawn legs, then butterfly prawns as directed above.

Sautéed Shrimp with Creamy Sesame Sauce

I developed this dish for a show entitled "New Chinese Cuisine." Chinese cooking doesn't normally use mayonnaise, but we use eggs, we use oil, and we use vinegar, so why not use them all together in mayonnaise? This is a uniquely delicious dish; combine it with vegetables and rice for a well-balanced meal.

Makes: 4 servings

Marinade

1	tablespoon Shao Hsing wine or dry sherry
2	teaspoons cornstarch
½	teaspoon salt
	Pinch of white pepper

■ ■ ■

¾	pound medium-size raw shrimp, peeled and deveined

Creamy Sesame Sauce

⅓	cup mayonnaise
2½	tablespoons rice vinegar
1	teaspoon sugar
2	teaspoons sesame oil

■ ■ ■

1½	tablespoons vegetable oil
2	teaspoons toasted sesame seeds
	Cilantro (Chinese parsley) sprigs for garnish

Preparation

Combine marinade ingredients in a medium bowl. Add shrimp and stir to coat. Let stand for 30 minutes.

Combine sauce ingredients in a medium bowl and set aside.

Cooking

Place a wok or wide frying pan over high heat until hot. Add oil, swirling to coat sides. Add shrimp and stir-fry for 2 minutes or until shrimp feel firm and turn pink. Pour sauce over shrimp and toss until shrimp are evenly coated. Transfer to a serving platter. Sprinkle with sesame seeds. Garnish with cilantro sprigs.

Sizzling Gingered Oysters

"Sizzling platter" dishes are quite popular in modern Chinese restaurants, and they are easy to serve at home. A saucy stir-fried dish is brought to the table, then poured onto a preheated metal platter, announcing its arrival with a loud sizzle and a puff of steam. If you don't have an appropriate platter, a small cast-iron skillet will do nicely. (Photo, page 140)

Makes: 2 servings

Sauce

1	**tablespoon chicken broth**
1	**tablespoon oyster-flavored sauce**
2	**teaspoons Shao Hsing wine or dry sherry**
1	**teaspoon soy sauce**
½	**teaspoon sesame oil**
	Pinch of white pepper

■ ■ ■

1	**jar (8 oz.) fresh oysters, drained**
½	**teaspoon salt**
1	**teaspoon cornstarch**
1	**tablespoon vegetable oil**
6	**thin slices fresh ginger**
2	**green onions (including tops), cut into 1-inch pieces**
½	**teaspoon cornstarch mixed with 1 teaspoon water**

Preparation

Combine sauce ingredients in a small bowl and set aside. Place oysters, salt, and cornstarch in a medium bowl and mix well. Set aside for 5 minutes.

Cooking

Bring 2 inches of water to a boil in a medium-size saucepan. Add oysters and cook for 1 minute or just until water returns to a boil. Drain well and set aside. Meanwhile, preheat a cast iron skillet or metal steak plate by placing over medium heat.

Place a wok or wide frying pan over high heat until hot. Add oil, swirling to coat sides. Add ginger and green onions and cook, stirring, for 1 minute. Add oysters and stir-fry for 30 seconds. Reduce heat to medium. Add sauce ingredients and cook for 1 minute. Add cornstarch solution and cook, stirring, until sauce boils and thickens. To serve, pour oysters on hot cast iron skillet or steak plate and serve immediately while still sizzling.

Tip: When oysters touch the hot plate, they will sizzle and may spatter slightly.

Eight-flavored Shrimp

Eight is a lucky number to the Chinese, so a lot of dishes are called "eight-flavored" even when they contain seven or nine flavoring ingredients. This one really does have eight major seasonings, all combined in a dry-fried shrimp dish.

Makes: 4 servings

1   **pound medium-size raw shrimp, peeled and deveined**
1   **tablespoon cornstarch**
¼   **teaspoon salt**

Pepper-salt Mixture
¼   **teaspoon salt**
¼   **teaspoon Chinese five-spice**
¼   **teaspoon ground toasted Sichuan peppercorns (optional)**
⅛   **teaspoon white pepper**

■   ■   ■

Vegetable oil for deep-frying
1   **teaspoon finely chopped shallot**
½   **teaspoon minced fresh ginger**
1   **teaspoon minced garlic**
1   **small fresh chili pepper, seeded and finely chopped**
     Shredded lettuce for garnish

Preparation

Combine shrimp with cornstarch and salt. Stir well and set aside for 10 minutes.

Combine pepper-salt mixture in a small bowl and set aside.

Cooking

Set wok in a ring stand and add oil to a depth of about 2 inches. Over high heat, bring oil to 360°F. Add shrimp, half at a time, and cook for 1 minute or until shrimp feel firm and turn pink. Lift out shrimp and drain on paper towels.

Remove all but 1 tablespoon oil from wok. Add shallot, ginger, garlic, and chili pepper and cook, stirring, until fragrant, about 5 seconds. Return cooked shrimp. Add pepper-salt mixture and cook, tossing to mix well, for about 30 seconds. Serve warm or at room temperature over shredded lettuce.

Tip: To lock in flavor, these shrimp are traditionally cooked in their shells, and the crunchy shells are eaten with the succulent meat.

Nesting Scallops

For special-occasion dishes, I like to present stir-fried dishes in a "nest" of crisp-fried shoestring potatoes. Seafood dishes are especially traditional this way — maybe it's the association with the swallows that nest on cliffs overlooking the sea.

Makes: 6 to 8 servings

6   **small dried black
     mushrooms**

Marinade
1   **tablespoon Shao Hsing wine
     or dry sherry**
2   **teaspoons cornstarch**
¼   **teaspoon salt**

■   ■   ■

1   **pound sea scallops, cut in
     half horizontally**
1   **large potato (about ¾ lb.)**
¼   **teaspoon salt**

Sauce
½   **cup chicken broth**
2   **tablespoons soy sauce**
2   **tablespoons oyster-flavored
     sauce**
½   **teaspoon sugar**

■   ■   ■

     Vegetable oil for deep-frying
1   **teaspoon minced fresh
     ginger**
1   **small red onion, cut into
     1-inch squares**
¼   **pound snow peas, ends and
     strings removed**
½   **cup sliced water chestnuts**
½   **cup sliced bamboo shoots**
2   **teaspoons cornstarch mixed
     with 4 teaspoons water**

Preparation

Soak mushrooms in warm water to cover for 30 minutes; drain. Cut off and discard stems and slice caps in half. Set aside.

Combine marinade ingredients in a small bowl. Add scallops and stir to coat. Set aside for 30 minutes. Peel potato and shred into a bowl. Add salt and cover with cold water. Set aside.

Combine sauce ingredients in a small bowl and set aside.

Cooking

Drain potato thoroughly and pat dry with paper towels. Set wok in a ring stand and add oil to a depth of about 2 inches. Over medium-high heat, bring oil to 360°F. Evenly spread half the of the potato over sides and bottom of a lightly oiled, 5-inch-diameter wire strainer. Press a second wire strainer of the same size down into the first to form a potato "nest." Holding strainers together, cook nest, carefully ladling oil over all sides for 2 minutes or until potato is evenly browned. Lift out, gently tapping strainers to loosen nest. Drain on paper towels. Repeat with remaining potatoes; set nests aside.

Remove all but 2 tablespoons oil from wok. Reheat oil over high heat until hot. Add ginger and cook, stirring, until fragrant, about 5 seconds. Add scallops and stir-fry for 2 minutes or until scallops turn opaque. Remove from wok and set aside. Add 1 tablespoon oil to wok. When oil is hot, add onion and mushrooms and stir-fry for 30 seconds. Add snow peas, water chestnuts, and bamboo shoots and stir-fry for 30 seconds. Add sauce and cook until heated through. Return scallops to wok. Add cornstarch solution and cook, stirring, until sauce boils and thickens. Place potato nests in center of platter and fill each nest with half of the scallop mixture.

Cashew Shrimp over Rice

When you are serving a number of dishes in a meal, the rice is always served separately, to be sampled between bites of the various dishes. But when you are making a meal of a single stir-fried dish, it's fine to serve it right on top of the rice, the way many a Chinese restaurant lunch is served.

Makes: 4 servings

Marinade
1   egg white, lightly beaten
2   teaspoons cornstarch
2   teaspoons Shao Hsing wine
     or dry sherry
¼   teaspoon salt
     Pinch of white pepper

■ ■ ■

1   pound medium-size raw
     shrimp, peeled and deveined

Sauce
¼   cup chicken broth
1   tablespoon Shao Hsing wine
     or dry sherry
1   teaspoon sesame oil
½   teaspoon sugar
¼   teaspoon salt

■ ■ ■

3   tablespoons plus 1 teaspoon
     vegetable oil
1   teaspoon minced garlic
1   teaspoon minced fresh
     ginger
¼   teaspoon crushed red pepper
½   cup frozen peas, thawed
1½   teaspoons cornstarch mixed
     with 1 tablespoon water
¾   cup unsalted roasted
     cashews
     Hot cooked rice

Preparation

Combine marinade ingredients in a medium bowl. Add shrimp and stir to coat. Set aside for 30 minutes.

Combine sauce ingredients in a small bowl and set aside.

Cooking

Place a wok or wide frying pan over high heat until hot. Add 3 tablespoons of the oil, swirling to coat sides. Add shrimp and stir-fry for 2 minutes or until shrimp feel firm and turn pink. Remove shrimp from wok. Add the remaining 1 teaspoon oil. Add garlic, ginger, and red pepper and cook, stirring, until fragrant, about 5 seconds.

Add sauce and peas; cook and toss for 30 seconds. Return shrimp to wok. Add cornstarch solution and cook, stirring, until sauce boils and thickens. Transfer to a serving dish. Sprinkle with cashews. Serve over rice.

Crystal Wrap

Not all Chinese food is meant to be eaten with chopsticks. In this New Year's dish, spoonfuls of diced shrimp and diced vegetables are rolled inside lettuce leaves to be eaten with the fingers. Lettuce is often used in the New Year's celebration to symbolize the offering of prosperity and good fortune. (Photo, page 157)

Makes: 8 servings

Marinade

1   **tablespoon Shao Hsing wine or dry sherry**
1   **teaspoon cornstarch**
¼   **teaspoon salt**

■   ■   ■

¾   **pound medium-size raw shrimp, peeled, deveined, and diced**
6   **dried black mushrooms**
2   **tablespoons vegetable oil**
1   **teaspoon minced fresh ginger**
1   **small carrot, diced**
½   **cup chicken broth**
½   **small zucchini, diced**
½   **cup diced water chestnuts**
2   **green onions (including tops), thinly sliced**
2   **tablespoons soy sauce**
⅛   **teaspoon white pepper**
½   **teaspoon cornstarch mixed with 1 teaspoon water**
½   **cup toasted pine nuts or coarsely chopped peanuts**
¼   **cup hoisin sauce**
8   **iceberg lettuce leaves**

Preparation

Combine marinade ingredients in a medium bowl. Add shrimp and stir to coat. Set aside for 30 minutes.

Soak mushrooms in warm water to cover for 30 minutes; drain. Cut off and discard stems and dice caps.

Cooking

Place a wok or wide frying pan over high heat until hot. Add oil, swirling to coat sides. Add ginger and cook, stirring, until fragrant, about 5 seconds. Add shrimp and stir-fry for 1½ minutes or until shrimp turn pink. Remove shrimp from wok. Add mushrooms, carrot, and broth and cook for 1 minute. Add zucchini, water chestnuts, and green onions and cook for 1½ minutes or until zucchini is crisp-tender. Return shrimp to wok and add soy sauce and pepper. Add cornstarch solution and cook, stirring, until sauce boils and thickens. Stir in pine nuts. Transfer to a serving platter. To eat, spread a little hoisin sauce on a lettuce leaf, spoon in some shrimp mixture, wrap lettuce around filling, and eat out of hand.

Tip: When a Chinese chef advises to match wedges with wedges, shreds with shreds, and cubes with cubes, he is passing along the age-old technique of cutting ingredients for one dish in the same shape. This facilitates even cooking and gives a pleasing appearance to the finished dish. In this classic presentation, ¼-inch dice is the desired size for cutting both the vegetables and shrimp.

甜品

DESSERTS

■■■

A sweet dessert does not automatically follow a Chinese meal the way it seems to in the West. Sometimes the meal ends with some fresh fruit; sometimes there is just a cup of tea, to let savory flavors linger. But for banquets and other special occasions, there may be fancy desserts.

Otherwise, the Chinese tend to serve sweet things apart from meals, with tea. Go to any Chinatown and you will see shoppers and local workers in bakery-cafes, sipping tea or coffee and enjoying traditional sweets like Steamed Sponge Cake (page 162). The same dishes are also popular in tea houses serving dim sum.

So it is mainly as a bow to Western customs that I finish with a chapter on desserts. Taking up the challenge, I offer a selection of both traditional sweets such as Sweet Rice Dumplings (page 168) and Almond Cream (page 165) and Chinese-inspired versions of Western desserts — for example, a Tianjin Trifle made with apricots and crystallized ginger (page 163), and Chocolate Tofu Ice Cream (page 161).

Mandarin Orange Rice Mold

What could be a more natural place to start with Chinese desserts than one made from rice? This is an elegant rice pudding, bound with an egg-yolk custard, lightened with meringue, and featuring one of China's favorite citrus fruits.

Makes: 8 servings

- 1½ envelopes (1½ tablespoons) unflavored gelatin
- ½ cup cold water
- 3 eggs, separated
- ⅔ cup sugar
- ½ teaspoon salt
- 2 cups hot milk
- 1 cup cold, cooked medium-grain rice
- 1 can (11 oz.) mandarin orange segments, drained
- 1 can (8¼ oz.) crushed pineapple, drained
- 2 teaspoons vanilla extract
- 1 cup whipping cream
- 1 tablespoon powdered sugar

Preparation

Sprinkle gelatin over cold water in a small bowl and let stand for 5 minutes to soften. Whisk together egg yolks, ⅓ cup of the sugar, and salt in a heavy 2-quart saucepan. Gradually whisk in hot milk. Cook custard, stirring constantly, over low heat until custard has thickened enough to lightly coat a metal spoon. Do not boil. Remove from heat; add softened gelatin and stir until dissolved. Add rice, oranges (reserving a few for garnish), pineapple, and 1½ teaspoons of the vanilla. Refrigerate until custard mounds slightly when dropped from a spoon.

In large bowl of an electric mixer, beat egg whites until frothy. Add the remaining ⅓ cup sugar, 1 tablespoon at a time, beating well after each addition. Continue to beat until sugar dissolves and meringue holds glossy, stiff peaks. Fold custard mixture into meringue. Spoon into a lightly greased 2½-quart mold. Cover and refrigerate for 4 hours or until firm.

To serve, unmold onto a dessert plate. Whip cream with powdered sugar and the remaining ½ teaspoon vanilla until soft peaks form. Garnish with whipped cream and reserved orange segments.

A Chinese New Year's menu. Clockwise from top: Buddhist Delight (page 72), Crystal Wrap (page 154), Red Envelope Fish (page 134), assorted New Year's candies ▶

Tianjin Trifle *(page 163);* ***Champagne Melon Balls*** *(page 169)*

158

Clockwise from right: *Sweet Rice Dumplings (page 168),* ***Honeydew Tapioca Delight*** *(page 167),*
Coconut Snow *(page 172)*

159

Chocolate Tofu Ice Cream

Puréed tofu takes the place of egg yolks in this rich-tasting but lower-calorie ice cream. (Photo, opposite page)

Makes: About 2 quarts

2   **packages (about 1 lb. each) soft tofu, drained**
2   **cups extra-rich milk or half-and-half**
1½   **cups sugar**
½   **cup vegetable oil**
4   **ounces (4 squares) semi-sweet chocolate, melted**
2   **tablespoons vanilla extract**
¼   **teaspoon salt**

Preparation

Blend all ingredients in a food processor or blender until smooth and creamy (it may be necessary to do this in several batches). Transfer mixture to a half-gallon or larger electric or hand-crank ice cream freezer. Assemble freezer according to manufacturer's directions, using about 4 parts ice to 1 part rock salt. When electric motor stalls or hand-cranking becomes difficult, remove dasher. Serve immediately, or transfer to a rigid plastic container, cover, and place in freezer for up to 1 month.

Sesame Almond Cookies

For extra color, use a mixture of black and white sesame seeds. (Photo, opposite page)

Makes: About 4 dozen cookies

2   **cups all-purpose flour**
¾   **teaspoon baking powder**
½   **teaspoon baking soda**
½   **pound lard**
⅔   **cup granulated sugar**
½   **cup packed brown sugar**
1   **egg**
¾   **teaspoon almond extract**
½   **teaspoon vanilla extract**
     Black or white sesame seeds
     Whole blanched almonds

Preparation

Sift flour with baking powder and baking soda and set aside. In a large bowl, beat lard with granulated sugar and brown sugar until fluffy. Add egg, almond extract, and vanilla extract and beat until well blended. Add flour to creamed mixture and blend thoroughly to form a soft dough. Cover with plastic wrap and refrigerate for at least 1 hour or up to 2 days.

To shape each cookie, roll about 1 teaspoon of dough into a ball. Roll in sesame seeds to coat evenly. Place balls 2 inches apart on ungreased baking sheets. Gently press an almond in center of each round.

Cooking

Preheat oven to 350°F. Bake in preheated oven for 8 minutes or until lightly browned.

161

Steamed Sponge Cake

When the Chinese first tried their hand at Western-style cakes, ovens were extremely rare in China, so they adapted them to other cooking methods. I think you will find this steamed cake every bit as light and delicious as the familiar baked variety. Besides its use in Tianjin Trifle (opposite page), it's popular as a snack with morning or afternoon tea.

Makes: One 9-inch round cake

1½   cups unsifted cake flour
½   teaspoon baking powder
½   teaspoon salt
6   large eggs, separated
1½   teaspoons grated lemon peel
1   teaspoon lemon extract
1   teaspoon vanilla extract
1⅓   cups sugar

Preparation

Grease a 9-inch springform pan and line the bottom with parchment or wax paper. Set aside.

Sift together flour, baking powder, and salt into a medium bowl. In small bowl of electric mixer, beat egg yolks for 1 minute or until thick and lemon-colored. Stir in lemon peel, lemon extract, and vanilla extract.

Using clean beaters, beat egg whites in large bowl of electric mixer until frothy. Gradually add sugar, beating well after each addition. Continue to beat until glossy peaks form. Sprinkle one-sixth of flour mixture over meringue. Using a rubber spatula, fold in flour just until blended, then fold in one-sixth of egg yolk mixture. Repeat, alternating flour and egg yolk mixture and blending well after each addition. Pour batter into prepared pan and spread evenly.

Cooking

Place bamboo steamer in a wok. Pour water to just below level of steamer and bring to a boil. Carefully set pan in steamer, making sure steamer is not tilted. Cover and steam, adding additional water if necessary, for 30 minutes or until a wooden pick inserted in center comes out clean. Serve warm or cold.

Tip: It is important to use a bamboo steamer; a metal steamer will allow too much condensation, causing the bottom of the cake to become soggy.

Tianjin Trifle

Tianjin, a port city near Beijing, was one of the major centers of Western trade and Western influence in the early twentieth century. So it seemed reasonable enough to name this adaptation of an English dessert after the city. (Photo, page 158)

Makes: 6 servings

Apricot Syrup

2   **cans (17 oz. each) apricot halves in heavy syrup**
¼   **cup apricot preserves**
¼   **cup finely chopped crystallized ginger**
¼   **cup apricot brandy or apricot liqueur**

    ■ ■ ■

1½ **cups whipping cream**
2   **tablespoons powdered sugar**
½   **teaspoon vanilla extract**
1   **Steamed Sponge Cake (opposite page)**

Preparation

Drain apricots, reserving 2 cups of syrup. Bring syrup to a boil in a saucepan and simmer until reduced to 1 cup. Add preserves and stir until melted. Stir in crystallized ginger and apricot brandy and cook for 1 minute. Set aside and let cool.

In a bowl, whip cream with sugar and vanilla until soft peaks form; set aside.

Slice sponge cake into strips about 1 inch wide. Arrange half of the cake slices on bottom of a 3-quart glass bowl.

Arrange half of the apricots on the cake. Drizzle half of the ginger syrup over cake and apricots. Spread half of the whipped cream over cake. Repeat with remaining cake, apricots, syrup, and whipped cream. Refrigerate overnight.

Tip: Purchased pound cake may be used in place of the sponge cake. This dessert should be made the day before serving to allow flavors to blend.

Autumn Fruit Salad

As summer gives way to fall, and the last melons sit alongside the first pears, I like to combine them in this luscious dessert. Asian pears, also known as apple pears or *nashi*, are now grown in this country as well as in Australia and New Zealand. Any firm pear can be substituted.

Makes: 6 servings

1	**can (11 oz.) lychees, drained**
1	**can (11 oz.) mandarin orange segments, drained**
1	**can (8 oz.) pineapple chunks, drained**
2	**cups honeydew melon balls**
1	**large Asian pear, cored and cut into chunks**

Dressing

2	**tablespoons lime juice**
1½	**tablespoons honey**
1	**tablespoon plum wine**
1	**tablespoon plum sauce**

■　■　■

Mint sprigs for garnish

Preparation

Combine all fruits in a bowl. Cover and chill. In a separate bowl, combine dressing ingredients. Cover and chill for 2 hours for flavors to blend. Just before serving, pour dressing over fruit and stir to mix lightly. Garnish with mint sprigs.

Tip: Asian pears are bursting with juice like a pear but crisp like an apple. You'll find several varieties in the market from yellow-green types with thin, tender skins to russet-colored types with slightly thicker skins. Peeling is optional; if you choose to do so, use a vegetable peeler so you remove only a very thin layer of skin.

Almond Cream

A sort of sweet soup, almond cream is sometimes served between courses at a banquet, like a fruit sorbet in a fancy Western meal. Similar desserts can be made from other nuts, particularly walnuts.

Makes: 8 to 10 servings

1	cup toasted whole almonds
6	cups water
½	cup uncooked long-grain rice, soaked overnight in 2 cups water
½	cup plus 1 tablespoon sugar
½	teaspoon almond extract
¼	cup toasted sliced almonds

Preparation

Place whole almonds and 1 cup of the water in a blender. Blend for 1½ minutes or until very smooth. Pour into a bowl and set aside.

Drain rice. Place rice and ½ cup of the water in a blender. Blend for 3 minutes or until smooth. Pour into another bowl and set aside.

Cooking

Bring the remaining 4½ cups water to a boil in a large saucepan. Add sugar and stir until dissolved. Reduce heat to medium. Add puréed rice and bring to a boil. Cook, stirring constantly, for 5 minutes or until soup thickens slightly. Stir in almond mixture and cook for 2 minutes. Remove saucepan from heat and stir in almond extract. Serve warm or at room temperature in individual soup bowls. Sprinkle with sliced almonds before serving.

Gold Coin Oranges

So many of the rituals surrounding the Chinese New Year have to do with prosperity. The New Year is also the time when oranges are at the peak of their season. So it's no surprise that oranges have come to symbolize gold, especially when sliced to resemble gold coins.

Makes: 4 servings

3   **oranges**
¼   **cup orange-flavored liqueur**

Syrup
½   **cup water**
¼   **cup sugar**
4   **thin slices fresh ginger**
1   **whole star anise (optional)**
    ■   ■   ■
2   **tablespoons chopped crystallized ginger**
    Mint sprigs for garnish

Preparation

Peel oranges and thinly slice crosswise. Combine orange slices and liqueur in a bowl and stir gently to mix. Cover and refrigerate for 2 hours or overnight.

Cooking

Combine syrup ingredients in a small saucepan. Bring to a boil, reduce heat, and simmer for 15 minutes. Discard ginger slices and star anise. Refrigerate syrup until very cold.

Drain liquid from orange slices, reserving 2 tablespoons of the liquid. Combine reserved liquid with syrup. Place orange slices in 4 individual serving bowls. Pour 2 tablespoons syrup over each serving. Sprinkle each serving with 1½ teaspoons crystallized ginger and garnish with a mint sprig.

Sweet Honeydew Tapioca Delight

The appearance of this dessert — cubes of honeydew melon in thick, translucent liquid the color of the palest jade — may seem odd at first, but you will be captivated by the subtly sweet flavor and smooth texture. (Photo, page 159)

Makes: 6 servings

2   tablespoons small tapioca pearls
4   cups water
½   cup sugar
1   cup puréed honeydew melon
¼   cup diced honeydew melon
6   tablespoons evaporated milk

Preparation

Soak tapioca pearls in warm water to cover for 5 minutes. Drain and set aside.

Cooking

Bring the 4 cups water to a boil in a medium saucepan. Add soaked tapioca and sugar and cook, stirring, for 5 minutes or until tapioca become translucent. Remove from heat and let cool. Stir in honeydew purée and refrigerate until chilled. Stir in diced honeydew. Transfer to six dessert bowls. Pour one tablespoon evaporated milk into each bowl. Serve cold.

Tip: Melons vary in sweetness, so taste the dessert before chilling and add a bit more sugar if desired.

Look for tapioca pearls in Oriental markets. They are larger than quick-cooking tapioca.

Sweet Rice Dumplings

Glutinous or "sweet" rice has a texture entirely unlike that of other rices. When ground to a flour and mixed with water, it makes an elastic dough that can be used to wrap other foods for frying, poaching, or steaming (see Golden Meat-filled Turnovers, page 43). Here it surrounds a nugget of sweetened peanut butter, and the dumplings are served in a peanut-based sauce. (Photo, page 159)

Makes: 24 dumplings

Filling
¼   **cup chunky peanut butter**
2   **tablespoons chopped unsalted peanuts**
2   **tablespoons packed brown sugar**

Dough
1½   **cups glutinous rice flour**
⅓   **cup boiling water**
5   **tablespoons cold water**

Sauce
⅔   **cup water**
½   **cup chunky peanut butter**
2   **tablespoons packed brown sugar**

Preparation

Combine filling in a small bowl. Mix well and set aside.

Measure glutinous rice flour into a bowl. Make a well in the center and pour boiling water into well, stirring with chopsticks or a fork, until dough is evenly moistened. Add cold water and stir, adding a few more drops if necessary, until dough forms a ball. On a lightly floured surface, knead dough for 5 minutes or until smooth and shiny. Cover with a damp cloth and let rest for 10 minutes. Roll dough into an 18-inch-long cylinder. Cut cylinder crosswise into ¾-inch pieces. Dust palms of hands lightly with rice flour and roll each piece into a ball.

To shape each dumpling, flatten one ball of dough with a rolling pin to make a 2½-inch circle; keep remaining dough covered to prevent drying. Place ½ teaspoon filling in center of circle. Gather and pinch edges together at the top to seal securely. Roll carefully between your palms to form a round ball. Cover filled dumpling with a damp cloth and repeat to fill remaining dumplings.

Cooking

In a large pot of boiling water, cook dumplings, stirring occasionally, for 5 minutes or until dumplings float on the surface. Lift out dumplings with a wire strainer and place in a colander to drain.

Combine sauce ingredients in a small saucepan. Bring to a boil over medium heat, stirring until smooth. Pour sauce onto a platter and place dumplings on top of sauce. Serve hot.

Champagne Melon Balls

For a dazzling dessert without a smidgen of fat, try these melon balls moistened with gingery champagne. The ginger syrup can be made well ahead of time and refrigerated; it's also good on ice cream. (Photo, page 158)

Makes: 4 servings

Ginger Syrup
½   cup water
2   tablespoons sugar
3   thin slices fresh ginger

■   ■   ■

½   cup each honeydew melon, cantaloupe, and watermelon balls
2   teaspoons chopped crystallized ginger
4   cups chilled champagne

Preparation

Place syrup ingredients in a small saucepan and bring to a boil. Reduce heat to medium-low. Cover and simmer for 15 minutes or until slightly thickened. Remove ginger slices. Let syrup cool, then cover and refrigerate until very cold.

To serve, divide melon balls evenly among 4 champagne glasses. Place ½ teaspoon crystallized ginger and 1 teaspoon ginger syrup in each glass. Fill each glass with champagne.

Martin Yan shopping for Chinese vegetables

170

Laughing Donuts

The Chinese name for these sesame-coated fritters is "Open Mouth to Laugh" because when they cook, each one "cracks a smile." I think you'll get a chuckle out of them, too.

Makes: 24 donuts

2	cups all-purpose flour
⅔	cup sugar
1	teaspoon baking powder
1	egg, lightly beaten
1	tablespoon lard, softened
3	tablespoons water
½	cup white sesame seeds
	Vegetable oil for deep-frying
	Powdered sugar (optional)

Preparation

Combine flour, sugar, and baking powder in a bowl. Gradually add egg, lard, and water. Knead gently until smooth. Wrap dough with plastic wrap and refrigerate for 2 hours. (If time is short, place dough in freezer for 30 minutes.) Roll dough into a 24-inch-long cylinder. Cut cylinder crosswise into 1-inch pieces. Roll each piece into a ball. Brush the surface of each ball with water, then coat with sesame seeds; set aside.

Cooking

Set wok in a ring stand and add oil to a depth of about 2 inches. Over high heat, bring oil to 340°F. Add sesame balls, half at a time, and cook, turning frequently with tongs, for 5 minutes or until balls crack open and turn golden brown. Lift out and drain on paper towels. Sprinkle donuts lightly with powdered sugar. Serve hot or at room temperature.

Tip: The donuts become crispier as they cool.

Coconut Snow

This light, creamy coconut pudding has come into mainstream Chinese cooking through the overseas Chinese communities of Singapore, Bangkok, and other cities in Southeast Asia. It is a popular dim sum item that can also serve as a refreshing ending to any meal, East or West. (Photo, page 159)

Makes: 6 servings

1½ envelopes (1½ tablespoons) unflavored gelatin
⅓ cup cold water
¾ cup boiling water
⅓ cup sugar
⅔ cup coconut milk
3 egg whites
1 tablespoon toasted shredded coconut

Preparation

Sprinkle gelatin over cold water in a medium bowl and let stand for 5 minutes to soften. Add boiling water, stirring, until gelatin dissolves. Stir in sugar and coconut milk. Let cool slightly, then refrigerate for 25 minutes or until lightly set. Place mixture in a food processor. Process for 30 seconds or until smooth. Remove to a bowl.

In a bowl, beat egg whites until they form stiff peaks. Fold egg whites into gelatin mixture. Pour mixture into an 8-inch square pan or 6 individual molds. Sprinkle coconut on top. Refrigerate for 3 hours or until firm.

Menu Planning

A great Chinese dinner is no accident; it is a carefully planned assortment of dishes which compliment each other in flavor, texture, and appearance. Fortunately, menu planning can be a simple and enjoyable task if you keep a few simple considerations in mind.

- The Occasion. Is it a formal sit-down banquet for ten or a stand-up buffet for thirty? A Sunday brunch for a group of friends or an intimate dinner for two? Each occasion calls for a different mood and a different menu.

- The Season. Take advantage of the freshest seasonal ingredients. Fruits and vegetables at the peak of their season have the most flavor and are usually at their least expensive. Use whatever fish and shellfish are freshest and best on the day you are shopping.

- Balance. No one element of flavor, texture, or color should dominate a meal. For example, a dinner composed of only hot and spicy dishes, or only dishes with red sauces, would quickly become boring. Include some dishes with firm, crunchy ingredients, others with smoother, more tender textures. Remember the five flavors — sweet, sour, salty, bitter, and hot — and try for an overall balance within the menu.

- Practicality. Consider the cooking methods required for each dish. For ease of preparation, as well as variety, select dishes that use different cooking techniques, preferably some that can be kept warm or finish cooking unattended. Imagine trying to complete three or four stir-fried dishes or steamed dishes at once!

Most of the recipes in this book serve four to six people in a Chinese-style meal. As a general rule, allow one dish per person (including soup) plus rice; to accomodate more people, either increase the number of dishes or double some of the recipes.

On these pages you will find several suggested menus based on the recipes in this book (dishes marked with an asterisk do not have a recipe here). The Index of Shows on pages 6-7 offers some other ideas. Use them as given or substitute other dishes as you like, and remember to let your own taste, creativity, and imagination be your guide in assembling your own delicious Chinese meals. Enjoy!

Beverages With Chinese Food

Tea is the all-time favorite Chinese beverage, although not necessarily at mealtime. In a formal meal, wines or other beverages accompany the foods, and the tea is served at the end of the meal, like coffee in the West. But many Chinese sip tea throughout their meals, as well as between meals.

Chinese teas are classified as green, black, or semi-fermented depending on how the leaves are processed. For black tea, the type most familiar in the West, the leaves are allowed to "ferment" before being dried, growing deeper in flavor and color (the process is not a true fermentation, but the action of enzymes within the tea leaves). Black teas are typically served between meals, as their flavor is too strong to go with most foods. Keemun and Lapsang Souchong are two well-known varieties. Green tea leaves are steamed or roasted immediately after picking, destroying the enzymes that cause the "fermentation" and resulting in a lighter, more refreshing brew. Dragon Well and Gunpowder are two excellent Chinese green teas; I also like a Japanese green tea flavored with roasted rice grains known as genmai cha. Semi-fermented, or Oolong, tea is given a shorter fermentation than black, and it falls somewhere between green and black in color and depth of flavor. This is the best type to accompany dim sum and other snacks. Ti Kuan Yin (Iron Goddess of Mercy) is an especially flavorful Oolong from Fujian Province. In addition to the three basic types, there are various teas flavored with chrysanthemum or jasmine flowers or lychee fruit.

A wide variety of tea is available in Chinese markets. Loose tea is less expensive than tea bags and keeps better. Store all quality teas tightly sealed in cans or jars and use within a few months after purchase for the best flavor and aroma.

Wine, at least Western-style grape wine, is not traditional in China, but many varieties can accompany Chinese meals. In most cases, one wine can be served throughout the meal. Champagne, either French or domestic, is a good choice with appetizers, and many people prefer to continue with the same wine with the following courses. Choose a bone-dry Brut or a sweeter Extra Dry according to your taste. Another all-purpose style of wine for Chinese meals is a semi-dry Chenin Blanc or

Riesling, which acts mainly as refreshment rather than competing for attention with the food.

When you want to highlight a particular dish or a particular wine, follow the same general guidelines as with Western foods: white wines with seafood, red wines with red meats, either with poultry and pork; full-flavored wines with strongly flavored foods, more delicate wines with delicate foods. For Chinese Blackened Fish, for example, a rich Chardonnay is a better match than a subtle Riesling, which would better accompany Poached Fish Fillets with Soy Dressing. Beef dishes such as Sichuan Tangerine Peel Beef, as well as most duck dishes, call for full-bodied reds such as Bordeaux, Zinfandel, Cabernet Sauvignon, or Merlot. Gewürztraminer, a white wine with a distinctive spicy aroma, goes well with Five-spice Broiled Pork Chops and Sichuan Boneless Chicken. Meats with sweeter sauces, such as Honey-glazed Garlic Ribs and Cantonese Barbecued Pork Ribs, call for a fruity red like Beaujolais. And China's own Shao Hsing rice wine, typically served warm like Japanese *sake*, goes especially well with "red-cooked" meats and other Shanghai-style dishes. Finding your own favorite combinations of food and wine can be a fascinating and delicious exercise.

Slightly sweet wines (or any other sweet beverages) help to "put out the fire" of chili-based foods. With really spicy foods, however, a cold beer (such as the excellent Tsingtao and Golden Dragon brands imported from China) is the most refreshing beverage, and many people prefer beer with most Chinese meals. Sparkling apple cider is a non-alcoholic alternative which is popular among many Chinese.

■ ■ ■

Here are some sample menus. Dishes marked with an asterisk are not included in this book.

■ EASY SUNDAY BRUNCH

Frittata with Barbecued Pork, 131   Vegetarian Cold Pasta, 64
Spinach Salad with Tofu Dressing, 83   Champagne Melon Balls, 169

■ DOWN HOME CHINESE COOKING

Steamed Pork Patty, 90
Chinese Broccoli with
  Oyster Sauce, 69

Steamed Rice, 46
Fresh oranges*

■ COCKTAIL PARTY BUFFET

Shrimp Toast, 24
Paper-wrapped Chicken, 22
Glazed Sesame Meatballs, 26
Champagne Melon Balls, 169

Baked Stuffed Mushrooms, 25
Golden Meat-filled Turnovers, 43
Quail Egg Siu Mai, 41

■ WEEK NIGHT SUPPER

Tomato Egg Flower Soup, 32
Steamed Rice, 46

Onion Beef, 103
Autumn Fruit Salad, 164

■ FRESH CRAB DINNER

Wonton Soup, 33
Steamed fresh asparagus*
Coconut Snow, 172

Crab with Ginger and Scallions, 144
Green Onion Pancakes, 27

■ OUTDOOR BARBECUE PARTY

Grilled Skewered Prawns, 23
Chinese Vegetable Pickles, 68
Steamed Sponge Cake,162, with
  strawberries and whipped cream

Qingdao Fajitas, 110
Watercress and Orange Salad, 84

■ SUMMER TAILGATE PARTY

Seaweed Rice Rolls, 28
Sesame Almond Cookies, 161
Five-flavored Watercress Salad, 85

Cantonese Barbecued Pork Ribs, 109
Glass Noodles with Peanut Sauce, 61

■ DINNER FOR EIGHT

Velvet Corn Soup, 29
Eight Treasure Noodle Pancake, 55
Red Envelope Fish, 134
Steamed Rice, 46

Rice in a Lotus Leaf, 47
Beef and Bean Curd Delight, 88
Stir-fried Winter Melon, 70
Tianjin Trifle, 163

■ COOKING WITH FRIENDS

Hakka Bean Curd Soup, 76
Mu Shu Vegetables, 81
Tomato Beef Fried Rice, 49

Honey-glazed Garlic Ribs, 92
Nesting Scallops, 152
Gold Coin Oranges, 166

■ SHANGHAI MENU

Red-cooked Lamb, 95
Crystal Wrap, 154
Steamed Rice, 46

Sweet and Sour Fish, 147
Chinese Vegetable Pickles, 68
Fresh fruit*

■ NORTHERN MENU

Mu Shu Vegetables, 81
Braised Cabbage with
  Bean Thread Noodles, 67
Steamed Rice, 46

Green Onion Pancakes, 27
Steamed Chicken with
  Garlic Sauce, 113

■ SOUTHERN MENU

Cantonese Roast Duck, 121
Stir-fried Winter Melon, 70
Sweet Honeydew Tapioca Delight, 167

Cashew Pork, 102
Tomato Beef Fried Rice, 49

■ SICHUAN MENU

Sizzling Rice Hot and Sour Soup, 35
Sichuan Boneless Chicken, 126
Dry-fried Green Beans with
  Minced Pork, 68

Spicy Pepper Beef, 101
Sichuan Braised Bean Curd, 75
Steamed Rice, 46

Make-ahead Sauces and Condiments

Many Chinese cooking methods, especially stir-frying, are already great kitchen timesavers. But when you are especially busy, having a couple of basic sauces made ahead of time can save a few more precious minutes. Except as noted, the following sauces will keep for a week or more in the refrigerator, tightly sealed in a jar. Add whatever combination of meat, poultry, seafood, or tofu and vegetables you like, and you have a nearly instant meal. Also included here are a few basic batters, flavored oils, and other condiments frequently used in Chinese cooking.

■ ALL-PURPOSE STIR-FRY SAUCE
A mixture of the basic seasonings used to flavor simple stir-fried dishes — ginger, garlic, and soy sauce. Add to the wok when the dish is nearly done.

Place a saucepan over high heat until hot. Add ¼ cup vegetable oil. Add 4 teaspoons minced garlic and 2 teaspoons minced fresh ginger and cook, stirring, until fragrant, about 5 seconds. Add ⅔ cup soy sauce, ⅓ cup Shao Hsing wine or dry sherry, and 2 tablespoons sesame oil and cook for 1 minute. Add 1 tablespoon cornstarch mixed with 2 tablespoons water and cook, stirring, until sauce boils and thickens. Makes about 1⅓ cups.

■ HOT AND SPICY STIR-FRY SAUCE
When you want a zestier, chili-spiked dish, stir this in to taste when the dish is nearly done.

Place a wok or medium saucepan over high heat until hot. Add 1½ tablespoons vegetable oil. Add 1 teaspoon each minced garlic and minced fresh ginger and cook, stirring, until fragrant, about 5 seconds. Add 1 tablespoon sliced green onion (white part only), ¼ cup each soy sauce, chicken broth, and Shao Hsing wine or dry sherry, and 2 teapoons hot pepper sauce or chili oil. Bring to a boil. Reduce heat to medium and cook for 2 minutes. Add 1 tablespoon cornstarch mixed with 2 tablespoons water and cook, stirring, until sauce boils and thickens. Let cool. Makes about ¾ cup.

■ SWEET AND SOUR SAUCE
May be added to stir-fries, but especially good with cubes of meat or fish fried in batter.

Place a medium saucepan over high heat until hot. Add 1 tablespoon vegetable oil. Add 1 teaspoon minced fresh ginger and cook, stirring, until fragrant, about 5 seconds. Add ¼ cup each orange juice and rice vinegar, 3 tablespoons each brown sugar and ketchup, 2 teaspoons soy sauce, and ½ teaspoon chili oil or hot pepper sauce and cook until sugar dissolves. Add 1½ tablespoons cornstarch mixed with 3 tablespoons water and cook, stirring, until sauce boils and thickens. Makes about 1¼ cups.

■ CHINESE SALAD DRESSING
Use whenever you want to give an Oriental flavor to salads of raw or cooked vegetables, cold meats, seafood, chicken, or whatever.

Combine ¾ cup rice vinegar, ⅓ cup soy sauce, ⅓ cup sugar, 1 tablespoon minced garlic, 1 tablespoon toasted sesame seeds, 2 teaspoons minced cilantro (Chinese parsley), and 1 teaspoon Chinese five-spice in a small bowl. Whisk in ⅔ cup vegetable oil and 3 tablespoons sesame oil. Makes about 2 cups.

■ SICHUAN SPICY SALT
Use in place of ordinary salt for seasoning meat and seafood dishes.

Place ¼ cup salt, ¾ teaspoon ground toasted Sichuan peppercorns, 1 teaspoon chili powder, and ¼ teaspoon white pepper in wok over medium heat, swirling wok, for 2 to 3 minutes. Let cool. Makes about ¼ cup.

■ CHILI OIL
Used in some of the recipes in this book; also popular in dipping sauces for dumplings, or as a table seasoning for a wide variety of foods.

Heat 1 cup vegetable oil in a small saucepan over high heat until oil reaches about 375°F. Remove from heat and add 1 tablespoon crushed red peppers and 1 tablespoon sesame oil. Let cool. Transfer oil to an airtight jar. Use as a dip or use a few drops to add zest to any dish. Makes about 1 cup.

■ FIVE FLAVOR OIL
Try this in dipping sauces in place of chili oil; or sprinkle a little into a dish at the end of cooking, like sesame oil; or use in cold dressings.

Heat 1 cup vegetable oil in a small saucepan over medium-high heat until oil reaches about 375°F. Add 3 crushed cloves garlic, 4 thin slices fresh ginger, 1 tablespoon sesame oil, ½ teaspoon whole black peppercorns, and ¼ teaspoon whole Sichuan peppercorns and cook for 10 minutes. Let cool, then strain out seasonings. Transfer oil to an airtight jar and store in refrigerator. Makes about 1 cup.

■ CANTONESE CRISPY BATTER MIX
Use this all-purpose batter for deep-frying foods such as shrimp, chicken, fish, or vegetables.

Combine ¾ cup all-purpose flour, 1¼ teaspoons baking powder, and 1 teaspoon sugar in a medium bowl. Gradually stir in ⅔ cup water. Blend in 2 teaspoons vegetable oil with wire whisk until smooth. Let stand for about 1½ hours before using. Makes about 1 cup.

■ CHINESE MUSTARD SAUCE
Can be used whenever Chinese or Dijon mustard is called for in a recipe. Gets mellower with time.

Combine ¼ cup dry mustard, 1½ tablespoons water, 1 tablespoon vinegar, ¼ teaspoon vegetable oil, and ¼ teaspoon sesame oil in a small bowl and stir to a smooth paste. Makes about ¼ cup.

■ RED-COOKING SAUCE
Also known as "Master Sauce," this can be used again and again for simmering meats or poultry, and it grows deeper in flavor with each use. Strain after each use and refrigerate or freeze.

Place a medium saucepan over high heat until hot. Add 2 tablespoons vegetable oil. Add 4 crushed cloves garlic and 6 thin slices fresh ginger and cook, stirring, until fragrant, about 5 seconds. Add 3 cups chicken broth, ½ cup soy sauce, ⅓ cup dark soy sauce, ¼ cup Shao Hsing wine or dry sherry, 2 whole star anise, 1 piece dried tangerine peel or 2 pieces fresh orange peel, and 3 tablespoons sugar. Bring to a boil. Reduce heat, cover, and simmer for 20 minutes, stirring occasionally. Strain liquid and use in braised, stewed, and casserole dishes. Makes about 3½ cups.

■ LOBSTER SAUCE
This sauce contains no lobster; instead, it contains the seasonings typically used in Cantonese lobster dishes. Try it with stir-fried prawns or chicken, or on steamed or poached fish.

Rinse ½ cup fermented black beans; drain. Mash beans in a bowl. Place wok over medium heat until hot. Add ¼ cup vegetable oil. Add 4 teaspoons minced garlic and cook, stirring, until fragrant, about 5 seconds. Add black beans, ⅓ cup Shao Hsing wine or dry sherry, ¼ cup each chicken broth and dark soy sauce, 2 tablespoons brown sugar, and 4 teaspoons sesame oil and cook for 2 minutes. Add 2 teaspoons cornstarch mixed with 4 teaspoons water and cook, stirring, until sauce boils and thickens. Use in steamed, stir-fried, or braised dishes. Makes about 1⅓ cups.

■ ALL-PURPOSE DIPPING SAUCE
Use as an all-purpose dipping sauce for fried seafood, meats, and vegetables.

Combine 1 cup ketchup, ½ cup soy sauce, ¼ cup each hoisin sauce and chicken broth, 2½ tablespoons sugar or honey, 1 tablespoon each Worcestershire sauce and sesame oil, 1 teaspoon chili oil, and ¼ teaspoon white pepper in a medium bowl and mix well. Makes about 2¼ cups.

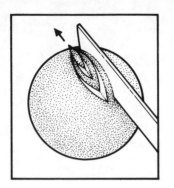
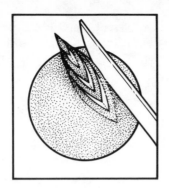

Apple Wings

1. Cut apple in half and place on cutting board. Make 2 diagonal cuts, angling the knife to form a small wedge. Place in lemon juice.

2. Cut out four more wedges, each ¼ inch wider than the previous wedge; place in lemon juice.

3. Place wedges together and gently move each slice to form layers.

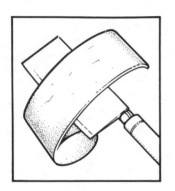
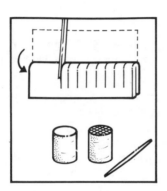

Daikon Chrysanthemum

1. Peel and cut daikon into 3-inch lengths. Soak in solution of 2 cups water and 2 tablespoons salt for 4 hours. With knife parallel to edge, cut a long continuous thin slice 6 inches long.

2. Fold sheet in half and make parallel cuts ⅛ inch apart. Cut a small ¾-inch-long cylinder from tip end of daikon and cut a crisscross pattern on one end.

3. Roll sheet around cylinder and secure with toothpick. Chill in ice water.

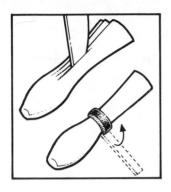

Green Onion Brushes

1. Trim root and green top. For single brush, slash top 2 inches repeatedly. For double brush, slide a ring of red chili pepper on onion and slash both ends.

2. Chill in ice water for at least 1 hour.

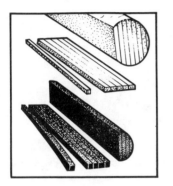

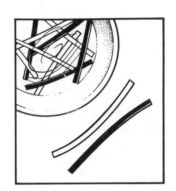

Carrot and Daikon Knot

1. Cut carrot and daikon into 6 x ¼-inch strips. Soak in solution of 2 cups water and 2 tablespoons salt until pliable.

2. Make a loop with a carrot strip. Weave daikon loop through carrot loop and pull ends to secure.

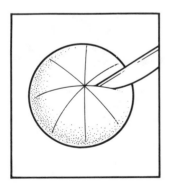

Tomato Flower

1. Place tomato stem side down. Cut skin across top and about two-thirds down sides. Repeat three more times to make eight segments.

2. Carefully lift tips of petals and separate skin from flesh.

181

Glossary

As I travel around the country teaching Chinese cooking, I like to do my own shopping for ingredients whenever I can. Fortunately, all styles of Asian cooking are growing in popularity, and most cities have at least one source of authentic Chinese ingredients. If there are no specifically Chinese stores in your area, try your local supermarket or health food store — more and more of them are stocking the ingredients listed on the following pages, and some have well-stocked Oriental sections.

Many of the canned, dried, and bottled ingredients vary widely between brands, so I recommend trying several different brands, if necessary, to find one which suits your taste.

BAMBOO SHOOTS	These edible shoots of bamboo plants have a slightly sweet flavor and crunchy texture. Available in cans, whole or sliced. Rinse before using, or blanch quickly if a tinny flavor persists.
BARBECUED PORK	Also called *char siu* in Chinese, these shiny red, highly seasoned pork roast strips are sold in Chinese take-out food shops. See page 109 for a recipe to make your own.
BEAN CURD	See Tofu
BEAN PASTE, SWEET	A thick sweetened purée of fermented soybeans, used as a seasoning in Sichuan and Hunan dishes. Don't confuse it with sweet red bean paste, which is made from Chinese red beans. Sweet bean paste is used as a filling for buns and pastries.
BEAN SAUCE, BROWN	A salty, pungent ground soybean condiment sold in cans or jars. Also referred to as yellow bean paste or sauce. Similar to Japanese *miso*. If labeled as just "bean sauce," this means the beans are still whole. It can also be purchased ground into a purée. Hot bean sauce is the same sauce with the addition of hot chili peppers.
BEAN SPROUTS	Tender white shoots with pale green hoods that are the sprouts of green mung beans. Sprouts from soybeans are sometimes available in Chinese stores. Purchase firm, white sprouts without brownish tails. They are best used the day of purchase. When stir-frying, cook briefly to retain crunchiness. Canned sprouts are not desirable.
BLACK BEANS, FERMENTED	These oval black beans, the size of currants, are salty and pungent. Before adding to other foods, rinse with water and lightly crush beans to release flavor. Sold in cans or in plastic bags. Because of their strong aroma, keep in an airtight container.
BOK CHOY	A vegetable of the cabbage family which is sometimes called Chinese chard. Stalks are long, smooth, and milk-white with a mild sweetness. Leaves are dark green and chard-like in appearance. When raw, the leaves have a hint of spicy hotness. Choose heads with bright white stalks and glossy leaves.

CABBAGE, CHINESE (NAPA)

Also known as Chinese celery cabbage. Grows in a long compact head with pale green leaves that have crinkled fringes. Slightly sweeter than head cabbage. Choose firm heads with crisp leaves that are free of browning.

CHICKEN BROTH

All recipes were developed using the Basic Chicken Broth recipe on page 30. If substituting canned chicken broth, you may wish to cut down on the amount of salt in the recipe.

CHILI OIL

A hot, reddish-orange oil infused with red chili. Used as a table condiment and sometimes as a flavoring ingredient in cooking. Available in various-size bottles. Easy to make at home (see recipe, page 179).

CHILI PASTE, CHINESE

Chinese markets sell an amazing array of hot sauces based on small dried chilies. Some are thickened with soybeans or sweet potatoes, and some contain a large amount of garlic. They also vary in intensity, so if you find one that is especially hot or mild, adjust the recipe amounts accordingly.

CILANTRO

Also known as Chinese parsley or fresh coriander. Aromatic herb with a unique aroma and flavor. Leaves are broad and flat with serrated edges. Choose perky bunches with fresh-looking leaves without browned edges. Store, standing in a jar of water, in the refrigerator, loosely covered with a plastic bag.

CORNSTARCH

See Starch

EGGPLANT, ORIENTAL

Slender, pale purple vegetable with fewer seeds, a thinner skin, and a sweeter taste than globe-shaped Mediterranean varieties. Choose firm ones with a taut, glossy skin and healthy-looking caps.

FISH SAUCE

A thin, salty, clear brown sauce used as an all-purpose seasoning. Has a fishy aroma at room temperature that mellows with cooking. Vietnamese call it *nuoc mam*. In Thailand, it is called *nam pla*. Available in bottles.

FIVE-SPICE, CHINESE

Cocoa-colored blend of five ground spices — star anise or anise seeds, cloves, cinnamon, fennel, and Sichuan peppercorns. Use sparingly as it has a pronounced flavor.

GINGER

Fresh: Sometimes called ginger root, this aromatic rhizome is an essential ingredient in Oriental cooking. Buy ginger with a firm feel and shiny skin. Peel before using.

Crystallized: Sugar-coated candied ginger made from stem or baby ginger which is less fibrous.

Preserved or Pickled: Peeled ginger slices packed in a clear liquid or in a light syrup in jars.

HAM, SMITHFIELD

A hard, salty, dry-cured ham from Virginia which is the closest equivalent to Chinese Yunnan ham. If unavailable, substitute any dry-cured ham such as prosciutto, Westphalian, or Serrano. All are available in most delicatessens.

HOISIN SAUCE	Thick, dark brown sauce with a sweet, spicy flavor that varies slightly between manufacturers. Usually made from fermented soybeans, flavored with spices, sugar, vinegar, garlic, and chili. Available in cans or bottles. Keep refrigerated after opening.
HOT BEAN SAUCE	See Bean Sauce, Brown
JICAMA	A large Mexican root vegetable with a thick brown skin. Hiding inside is a sweet white flesh that resembles water chestnuts in flavor and texture. Choose firm, well-formed smaller ones (no larger than a grapefruit), as larger ones tend to be more fibrous.
MUSHROOMS	Unless otherwise noted, "mushroom" means the familiar cultivated type. Other mushrooms are identified by name, including the following: *Dried Black*: Also known as *shiitake* in Japanese. Rich, meaty-flavored mushroom with a wide flat cap. Look for the ones with a lacy system of cracks on the surface of the cap and a creamy-colored underside. Before using, soak in warm water for 30 minutes; drain and cut off and discard stems. They keep well, so buy in bulk for the best price. Fresh shiitakes do not have as much flavor. *Enoki*: A small, delicate mushroom of Japanese origin, with a white stem and a small bulbous cap. Gaining popularity and availability, they are sold fresh in small bags and are now available in many supermarkets. *Straw*: Light brown, with bulb-like caps resembling a partially opened umbrella. Grown in beds of rice straw, they have an unusual slippery texture. Available from China in cans.
MUSTARD, CHINESE	Hot, pungent table condiment made from a combination of ground white and dark mustard seeds. Sold in jars. To make your own, use a good brand of powdered mustard and an equal part of water; or try the recipe on page 179.
NOODLES	The Chinese word mein covers a wide range of wheat-flour noodles, fresh or dried, with egg or without. If there is a Chinese noodle factory in your area, you may be able to choose among many types of fresh noodles. Some supermarkets carry similar Japanese-style fresh noodles, usually alongside the tofu. Use the thinnest fresh noodles you can find, or substitute a thin Western-style pasta such as tagliarini or vermicelli.
OYSTER-FLAVORED SAUCE	Thick, dark brown sauce made from an extract of oysters, sugar, salt, caramel, and starch. Thickness and seasoning varies among manufacturers. Available in bottles and cans. Keep refrigerated after opening.
PEPPER	Both black and white peppers are used in Chinese cooking. The latter has the dark husk removed and is used in light-colored dishes where flecks of black pepper would be undesirable.

PEPPERCORNS, SICHUAN

Not a true peppercorn, but the dried berry of an unrelated plant. Quite different from black pepper, with a pronounced aroma and pleasant numbing (not peppery-hot) flavor. To bring out the flavor, toast in a frying pan over medium heat for 5 minutes or until fragrant, shaking pan frequently. If recipe requires ground toasted Sichuan peppercorns, use a mortar and pestle to grind to a fine powder. Available in pouches and jars.

PLUM SAUCE

A spicy sauce with a jam-like consistency made from salted plums, vinegar, sugar, and chili. Consistency and taste varies among manufacturers. Available in cans or jars.

PRESERVED VEGETABLES, SICHUAN

Also called *jah choy*, this hot and spicy pickle of kohlrabi or radish is used in a variety of Sichuan and Mandarin dishes. Sold in cans or from large earthenware pickling crocks in Oriental markets. For a milder flavor, rinse off some of the red chili powder, then slice.

RED CHILI PEPPER, DRIED

Several dishes in this book call for whole dried chilies. They are typically used to season the oil in a stir-fried dish, then discarded. Any small dried chili from China, Mexico, or Southeast Asia can be used. They are much less expensive when bought in bulk rather than in small spice jars. "Crushed red pepper" is the same thing chopped into small flakes.

RICE

Rice comes in many varieties and shapes, including long, medium, and short grains. Which to use is largely a matter of taste and habit. In general, the longer the grain, the more firm and separate the rice cooks; the shorter types cook to a softer, stickier consistency. Chinese cooks never use parboiled (converted) rice or "instant" rice.

Long-grain: This rice is a kitchen staple in the southern regions of China. When cooked properly, the grains are separate and fluff easily with a chopstick or fork. It is the best for fried rice dishes. The California-grown Hinode variety is ideal - fluffy and flavorful when cooked.

Medium-grain: Grown mostly in California, this slightly chewy rice closely resembles long-grain and is a nice compromise between firm and soft, separate and sticky.

Glutinous (Sweet): This is a type of short-grain rice which is pearly and slightly transparent when cooked. It requires less water when cooking and is usually steamed rather than boiled. Because of its sweetness and stickiness, it is commonly mixed with other ingredients for use in stuffings or dessert puddings.

SAUSAGE, CHINESE

Also called *lop cheong* in Cantonese, these sausages are made with either pork and pork fat or pork and duck liver. They are seasoned with salt, sugar, and wine and have a sweet, full-bodied taste. Sold in six-inch links tied together in pairs. They can be stored for a long period of time in the freezer.

SESAME OIL

An amber-colored, strongly flavored, aromatic oil pressed from toasted sesame seeds, this should not be confused with the cold-pressed sesame oils sold in health food stores. It is used to flavor a hot cooked dish just before serving, or as a flavor ingredient in marinades or soups. Purchase in glass, rather than plastic bottles. Refrigerate after opening.

SESAME SEEDS	There are two varieties, black and white. The white are hulled and have a sweet, nutty flavor. To bring out the flavor, toast briefly in a dry frying pan over medium heat, shaking pan occasionally, until fragrant and golden. Black sesame seeds are slightly more bitter and are called *goma* in Japanese. Keep in an airtight container.
SHAO HSING WINE	See Wine
SHRIMP, DRIED	These are small shrimp that have been preserved in a salty brine, then dried. Their strong fishy flavor is used to enhance vegetable dishes and soups. Before using, soak in warm water for about 30 minutes to soften. Available in plastic bags. Keep refrigerated in an airtight container.
SNOW PEAS	Also called sugar peas or Chinese pea pods. A special variety with flattened pods picked before the seeds mature; the whole pod is edible and has a sweet taste and crisp texture. Select medium-size, stiff pods with bright green color and no yellowing. Before using, snap off ends and string lengthwise. Frozen pea pods are a bit too soft for stir-frying.
SOY SAUCE	Good soy sauce is an essential ingredient in Chinese cooking. Its rich, salty, slightly tart flavor makes it a versatile seasoning for all kinds of foods.
	Cantonese soy sauces are classified as light and dark, depending on thickness and depth of flavor. Unless otherwise specified, the recipes in this book call for all-purpose Kikkoman soy sauce. Kikkoman, manufactured in the United States, is the most commonly available soy sauce in the market, with similar color to Cantonese light soy, but much less salty. There is also a reduced-sodium version, Kikkoman Lite, which can be used in equal proportions but contains 40% less sodium. Kikkoman Lite contains only about 7% sodium as compared to 22 to 24% sodium in most Chinese brands of soy sauce. Read soy sauce labels carefully. Naturally brewed soy sauces (like Kikkoman and any from the Orient) are made entirely by fermentation from soybeans, wheat, salt, and water. There are some brands of soy sauce made from chemically hydrolyzed vegetable protein and are artificially colored with caramel — these are not recommended.
	Dark soy sauce is thicker and darker due to the addition of molasses. It is used in certain stews and other dishes where a richer, deeper color and flavor are desired. There is no domestic or Japanese equivalent, so most dark soy sauces in our markets come from Hong Kong or China. Labels can be confusing, but if it contains molasses, it's dark soy sauce. You can also identify light and dark soy sauce by appearance. When swirled in the bottle, light soy drains quickly, while dark soy leaves a dark brown, slowly draining stain.
	After opening, all soy sauces tend to darken and become more concentrated with time. Refrigerate to prolong shelf life.
STAR ANISE	Brown, eight-pointed, star-shaped seed pods with a strong licorice flavor, often used in stews and braised dishes. If recipe calls for one star anise, an equivalent of broken points will do, as it is hard to find a plastic bag of whole ones.

STARCH	Cornstarch, tapioca starch, and arrowroot starch are good thickening agents for making a clear, shiny sauce. Combine one part starch with two or three parts cold water and slowly add to cooking liquid. Cornstarch tends to settle, so always stir mixture just before adding.
TANGERINE PEEL, DRIED	The dried peel of a tangerine, it has a sweet citrus smell and pungent flavor. Soak briefly to soften before using. Available in small cellophane packages. Fresh orange peel may be substituted.
TOFU	The Japanese name for a highly nutritious product also known as bean curd. A "milk" extracted from soybeans is curdled and drained in a process much like making cheese.

Fresh: Fresh tofu has a creamy-white color, a smooth and custard-like texture, and a bland taste. Most commonly sold in sealed plastic tubs, it is also available in vacuum-packed pouches or foil-lined cartons which can be stored at room temperature. Refrigerate fresh tofu and vacuum-packed tofu after opening, preferably covered with cold water. If water is changed daily, tofu will keep for up to a week. Discard if a strong odor develops.

Tofu may be labeled firm, medium, or soft. Only firm and medium are used in the recipes in this book; the former holds its shape well in stir-fried and braised dishes, while the latter is softer, more crumbly, and more suitable for soups.

Dried: These are packed in sheets (used as a wrapper) or sticks (used in braised dishes).

Fermented: Sold in jars with a thin liquid; may have chilies added for color and flavor. It has a strong aroma and flavor like some aged cheeses. Store in refrigerator.

Pressed or Fried: This type of bean curd is available in compact, golden brown cakes of pressed and deep-fried tofu, sometimes seasoned with five-spice. Sold in pouches. Used for its chewy, meaty texture, mainly in stir-fried dishes. Store in refrigerator.

VINEGAR, RICE	Chinese rice vinegars come in several colors and flavors, but as used here, "rice vinegar" refers to the clear or "white" variety. Japanese rice vinegar is widely available and very good. Be sure to get the unseasoned variety. Chinkiang vinegar is a dark brown and richly colored "black" vinegar from eastern China.
WATER CHESTNUTS	Fresh water chestnuts from Oriental markets have dark brown scaly skins with white, crunchy-sweet interiors. Choose firm ones free of wrinkles and mold. Peel just before using and place in water to prevent discoloration. Canned water chestnuts, whole or sliced, are more readily available. Rinse before using, or blanch quickly if a tinny flavor persists.
WINE, SHAO HSING	A Chinese wine made from fermented rice, Scotch-colored and slightly sweet with a nutty flavor. Dry sherry is a closer substitute than sake (Japanese rice wine). Shao Hsing wine is available in Chinese markets.
WRAPPERS	Chinese love to enclose bits of food in wrappers, so there are many shapes and types to choose from. When using wrappers, avoid undue exposure to air, or cover them with a damp cloth to prevent drying. Many types are available in supermarkets in the produce section. Two types are used in this book: wonton wrappers, thin 3½-inch squares; and siu mai wrappers, the same size but round. They usually come fresh, in one-pound packages. All wheat-flour based wrappers freeze well.

INDEX

MANY THANKS TO YOU,
MY READERS AND VIEWERS,
AND TO ALL THOSE WHO HAVE
SUPPORTED THIS PROJECT
AND THE YAN CAN COOK SHOW:

HINODE

 **KIKKOMAN**

MEYER®
Le COOK'S-WARE

Yan Can & Company offers
a selection of additional gourmet
merchandise. For details write:
**Yan Can & Company, P.O. Box 4755
Foster City, CA 94404**